Gabriel Koeppen

Cello Method

Have fun playing the Cello

Lesson Book 1
with online material (audio/pdf)

ED 22501D
ISMN 979-0-001-21562-6
ISBN 978-3-7957-2562-4

Revised edition 2022
with musical terms in
British and American English

SCHOTT

www.schott-music.com

Mainz · London · Madrid · Paris · New York · Tokyo · Beijing

Impressum:

Order number: ED 22501D
ISMN 979-0-001-21562-6
ISBN 978-3-7957-2562-4

Recording: Markus Gierke, Flensburg
Violoncello and arrangements: Gabriel Koeppen

Cover photo: Monika Remus, Flensburg
English translation: Julia Rushworth
Typesetting and layout: Jan Willems, Villingen-Schwenningen
Editor: Dr Rainer Mohrs

Printed in Germany · BSS 57494

Contents

Welcome

'The cello is a classical instrument!' – that's what you learn at school and that's what you find in most tutorial books. Is it true, though?

Music of any style can be played on the cello. With this book you can play great pieces from the classical, folk, rock and jazz repertoire, right from the start. You can play almost all the pieces as a duet with your teacher or with the play-along tracks. Whether you go on later to play in a symphony orchestra, chamber ensemble or band, you will have a lot of fun and make a lot of new friends.

To get there you'll need a good teacher (don't try to manage by yourself) and a bit of patience. Success in sport requires regular training – and this applies to learning an instrument, too. If you play a little every day you will make rapid progress. Set out a practice timetable and soon it will become part of your routine, like eating and drinking, sport, reading, computer, homework and other activities.

Below many of the pieces you will find the symbol D: D this means you can download an additional piano accompaniment or a 3rd cello part as a free PDF file; there are even a few quartet versions for ensemble playing. On the website www.schott-music.com enter order number ED 22501D or the name of this Cello Method and select individual files from 'Further Information' – 'Downloads', where you can open and print them.

Here are a few tips on playing with the tracks:

Practise each piece without the recording first, until you feel confident.
2. If you want to play along with the play-alongs later, start by just listening to the piece on the recording.
3. Tune your cello carefully. Use the tuning notes on tracks 77-80 or a tuning device (A = 441).
4. Each piece has a two-measure (bar) count-in. If a piece begins with an upbeat the count-in is correspondingly shorter.
5. Almost all the pieces can be heard in two versions: once with the cello part and once without. The jam tracks are recorded without cello.
6. Most pieces have been recorded without repeats to save time (even where a repeat is marked for playing duets).

Enjoy your practice!

Gabriel Koeppen

Please visit **www.schott-music.com/online-material** to download all audio files for free using the following voucher code:
sN2ZUhDG

Key to symbols:

T = refers to Tune book

i = useful practice tips

L = extra tips for lessons

= writing practice

D = additional material available to download

To my fellow cello teachers

This method is designed for beginners on the cello and is suitable for adult beginners, too. The first book deals with notes in 1st position.

'All roads lead to Rome' – and that saying may also be applied to cello teaching, too. Each pupil learns differently and every teacher has their own methods, tricks and ruses. A good teacher does not simply stick to a fixed teaching plan, but adapts to the individual needs of each pupil. In my opinion there is no single ideal method for learning – and this applies to my cello tutorial method, too.

I have based this method on the following principles:

1. Right from the beginning, the student should be motivated by playing along with the teacher and the play-along tracks.
2. My initial priority is developing good bow control and listening skills, so we start with simple rhythms and limited string crossing.
3. The student starts with placing the 2nd finger: this keeps the hand fairly steady and reduces the risk of twisting.
4. In order to understand fingerings the student starts by learning all the notes in first position, with no sharps or flats. New notes are introduced as we explain music theory.
5. Little writing exercises encourage and reinforce learning to read music.
6. Simple improvisation pieces ('Jam tracks') are designed to stimulate composition and improvisation skills.

Please use this book **flexibly**, for example:

- If you want to start with the first finger, simply skip a lesson and start on page 22.
- If you'd rather learn to use one finger *on all the strings*, add appropriate pieces, for instance from my book 'Hot Cello 1'.
- If a piece seems too difficult, just skip it and come back to it later.
- Heartfelt thanks go to all the pupils and colleagues who have helped me work on this book.
- I am always grateful for suggestions. I hope you will have fun working through this cello method.

Best wishes,

Gabriel Koeppen

Holding the Cello

- Find a chair (or stool) with a flat horizontal seat.
- Sit at the front of the seat.
- The chair should be high enough so your thighs are horizontal or, preferably, slope downwards slightly.
- Place the cello spike on the floor slightly to the right, so that the scroll doesn't get in your way. Use an endpin anchor if necessary.
- rest the C bouts at the sides against your knees and tilt the cello slightly to the right.

Things to remember:

The Cello

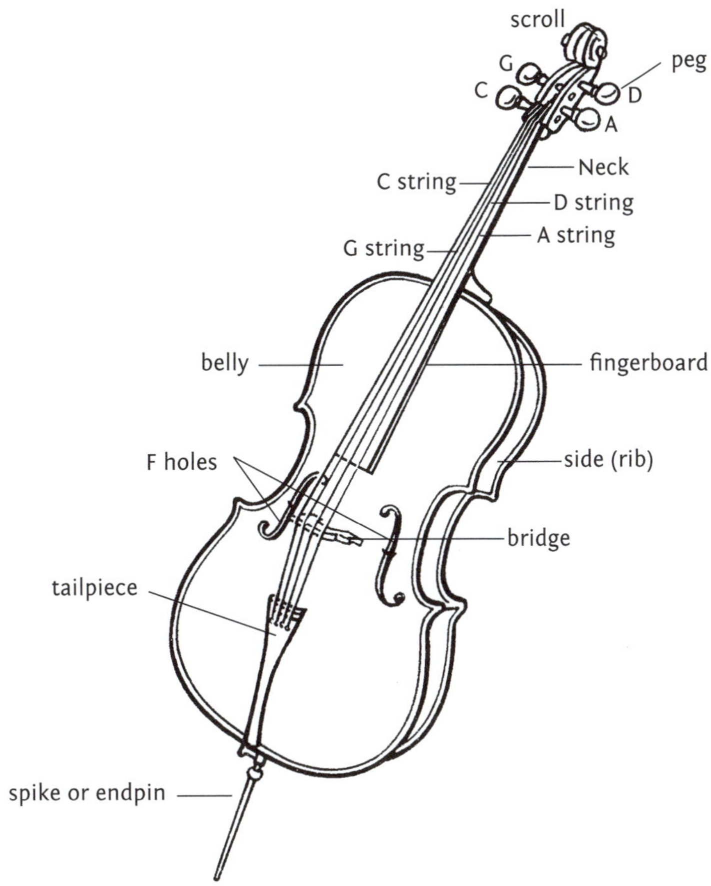

The Bow

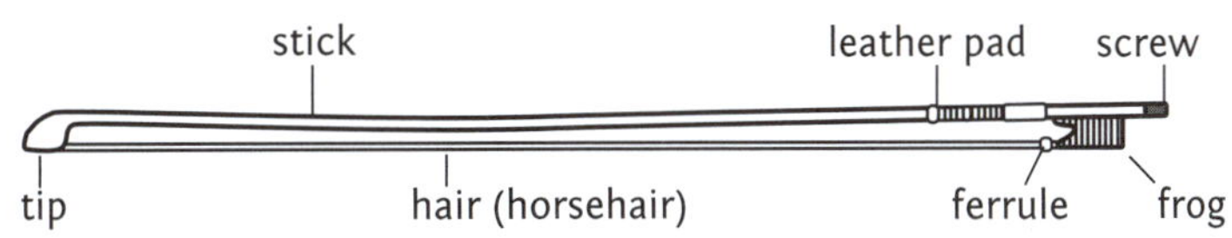

Musical notation

The stave

A stave consists of five lines. The notes can be written either on the lines or in the spaces between them.

These notes are on the lines:

These notes are in the spaces;

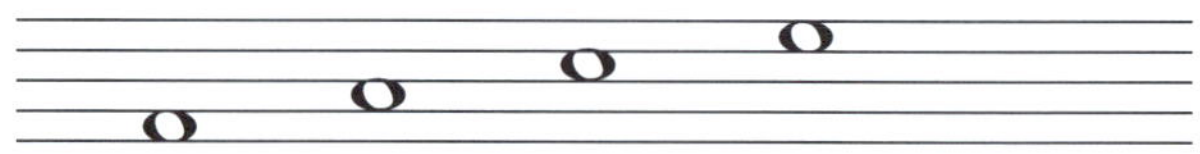

Leger lines

Sometimes the stave doesn't go far enough. Then we simply draw little **leger lines**:

going above the stave

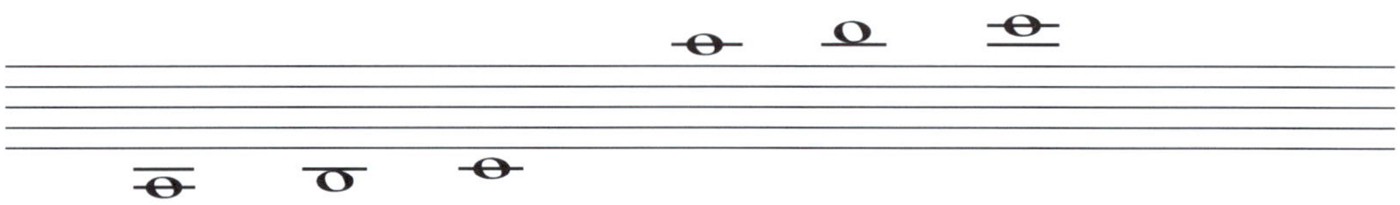

going below the stave

Clefs

At the beginning of each stave is a **clef**. This determines pitch. Music for low-pitched instruments such as the cello, double bass or tuba is usually written in the **bass clef.** The dots on the bass clef go on either side of the line representing F – so it is also called the F clef.

Bass or F clef

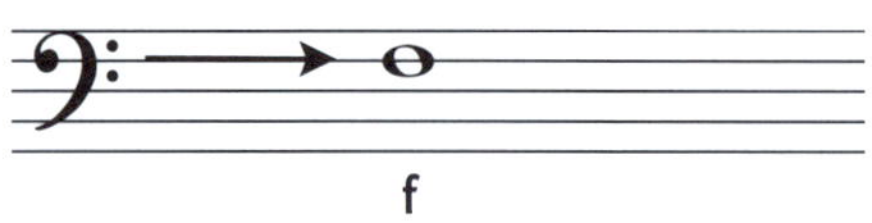

Higher sounding instruments such as violin or flute are usually written in the treble clef, which curls around the note G – so it is also called the G clef.

Treble or G clef

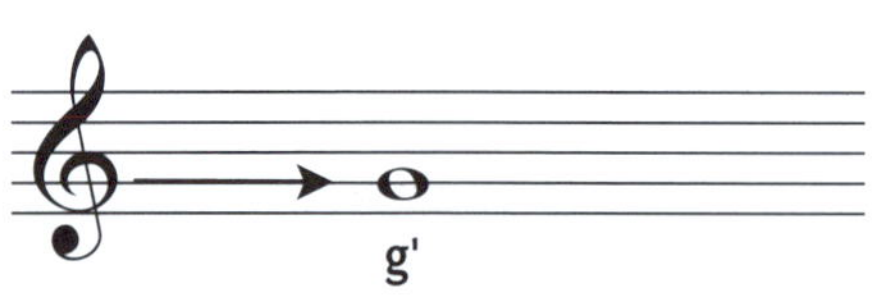

Introducing note values

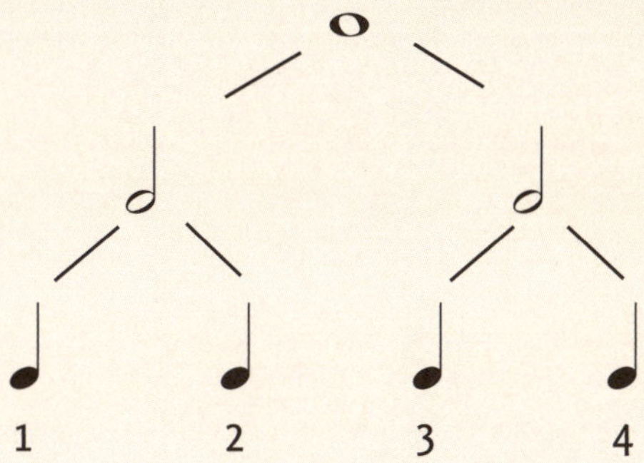

A **whole note (semibreve)**
is four beats long

A **half note (minim)**
is two beats long

A **quarter note (crotchet)**
is one beat long

Measures (bars) and time signatures

To make a piece of music easy to read, it is divided into measures (bars). A bar is a small musical unit between two measure (bar) lines. Measure (bar) lines will help you put accents in the right places, too: the first note in each measure (bar) normally has the strongest accent. The time signature is given at the beginning of a piece. In this book we start with 4/4 time (4 quarter notes (crotches) in a measure (bar)).

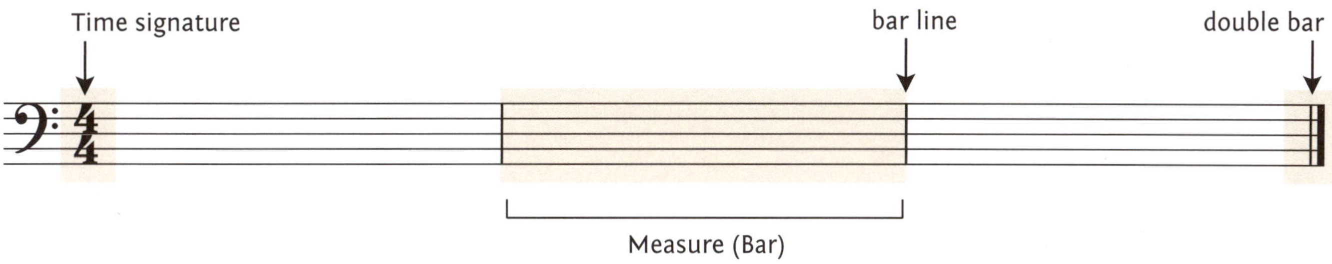

Exercises

Write whole notes (semibreves) on the lines:

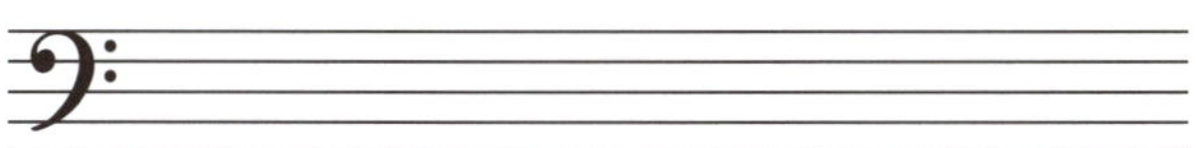

Write whole notes (semibreves) in the spaces:

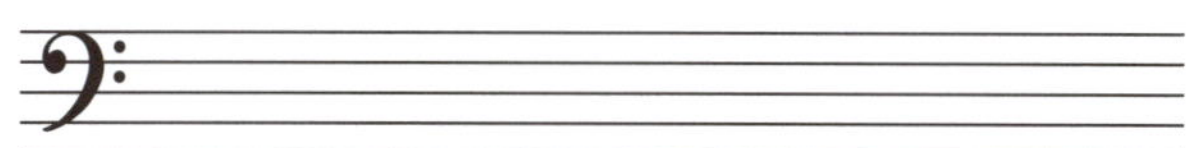

Add adjacent notes, going upwards and downwards. How far can you go?

Fill in the missing note values:

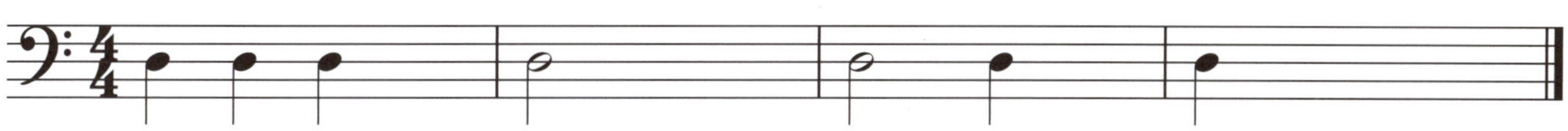

Open strings

Plucking the strings (pizzicato)

Put the bow down for a while. Use your right index finger to pluck strings like a double bass player. Rest your thumb gently on the lower side of the fingerboard. After plucking, you can place your index finger on the next string.

Pluck the G string. You can speak or sing along with the cello note:

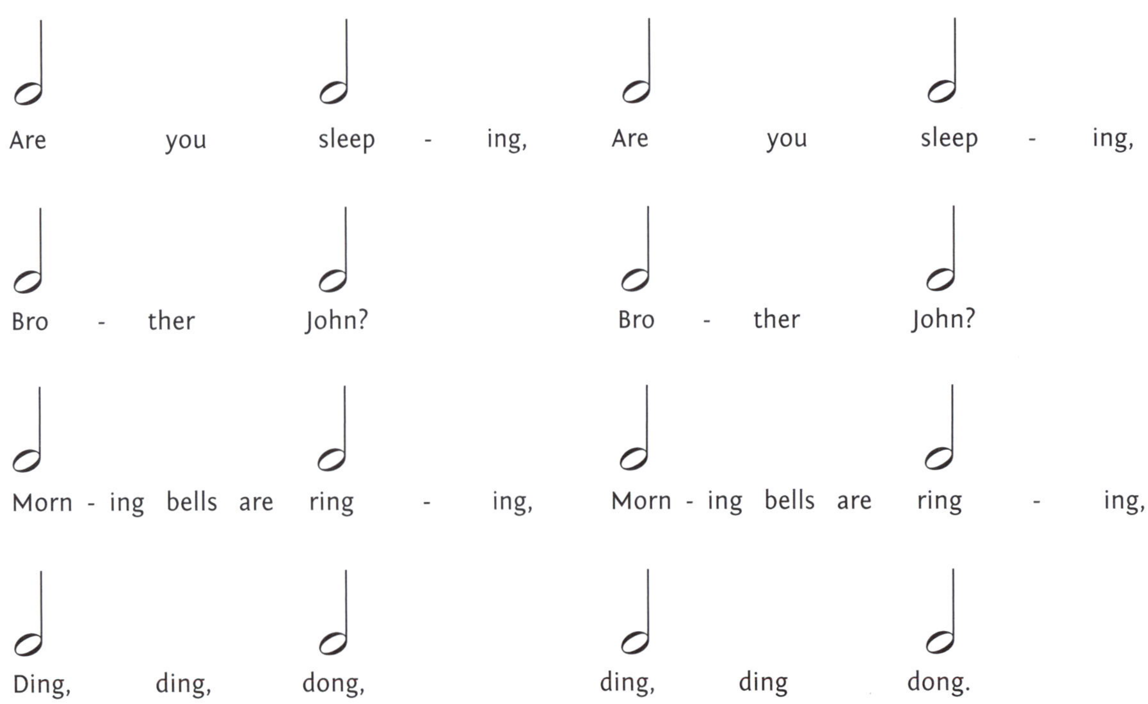

Repeat on all the strings.

Half note (minim) 𝅗𝅥 = 2 beats

Quarter note (crotchet) ♩ = 1 beat

Hey, ho, hitch the cart up now

Canon
English translation:
Julia Rushworth

Repeat sign: :‖

There's a bug upon the wall

Playing with the bow

How to hold the bow:

1. Hold the stick with your left hand near the middle, with the frog pointing to the right.
2. Let your right hand hang loosely over the frog. Place your middle finger on the metal ring and your thumb in the angle between the frog and the stick: the thumb should sit there, not poke through.
3. The other fingers rest loosely on the stick, with the index finger on the leather binding.

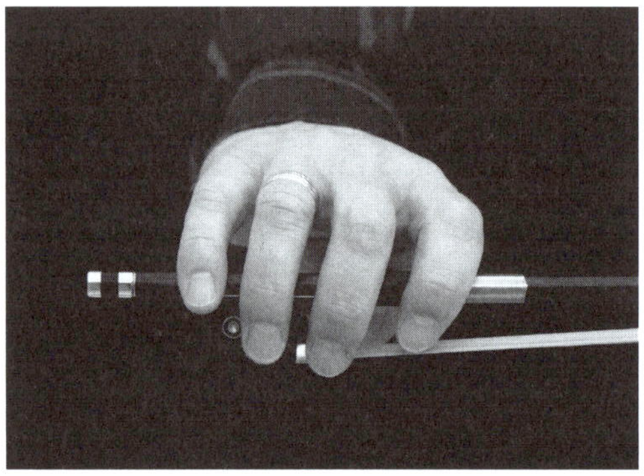

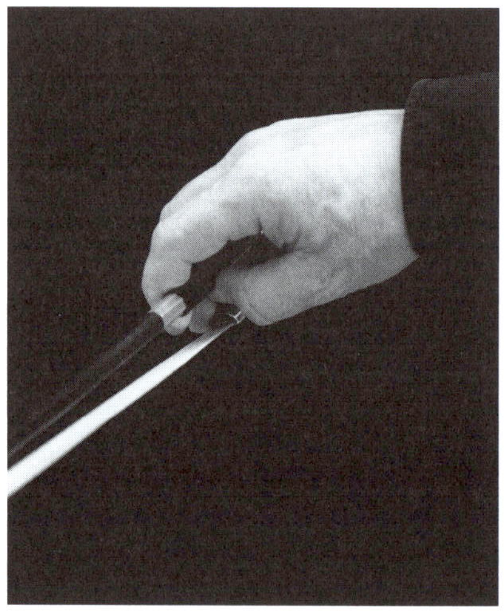

How to play with the bow:

1. Move the bow between the bridge and the fingerboard. Tone quality depends on the point of contact, bow pressure and bow speed.
2. Try to play straight bows; that means moving the bow at right angles to the string.
3. Bowing involves moving the shoulder, elbow and wrist. The nearer you move towards the point, the more the lower arm opens out.

Things to remember:

Try playing tunes you know on one string, for example:

Brother John
Merrily We Roll Along
O when the saints
Twinkle, twinkle, little star
Old MacDonald had a farm
Go tell Aunt Nancy

What other tunes do you know?

____

____

____

Whole note (semibreve) o = 4 beats

⊓ = **down bow**: move towards the point
v = **up bow**: move towards the heel

Pluck the notes first, then use the bow!

Track 1

Thoughtful

G. K.

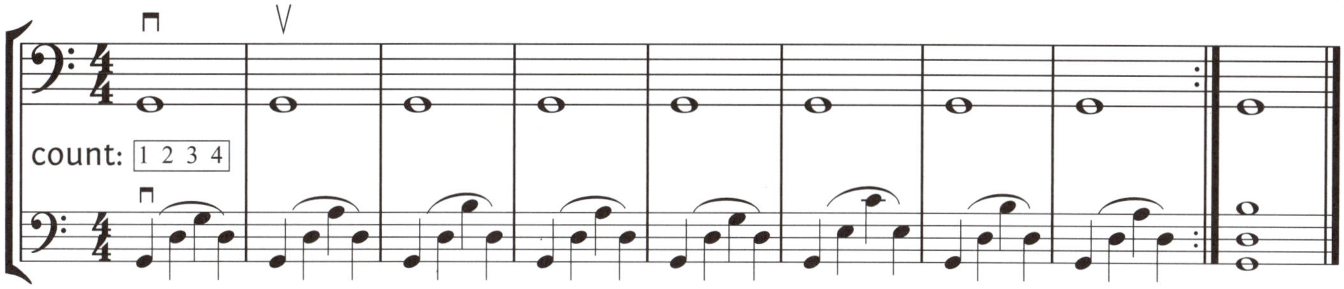

Track 2

Waking up

G. K.

Track 3

One-note Rock

G. K.

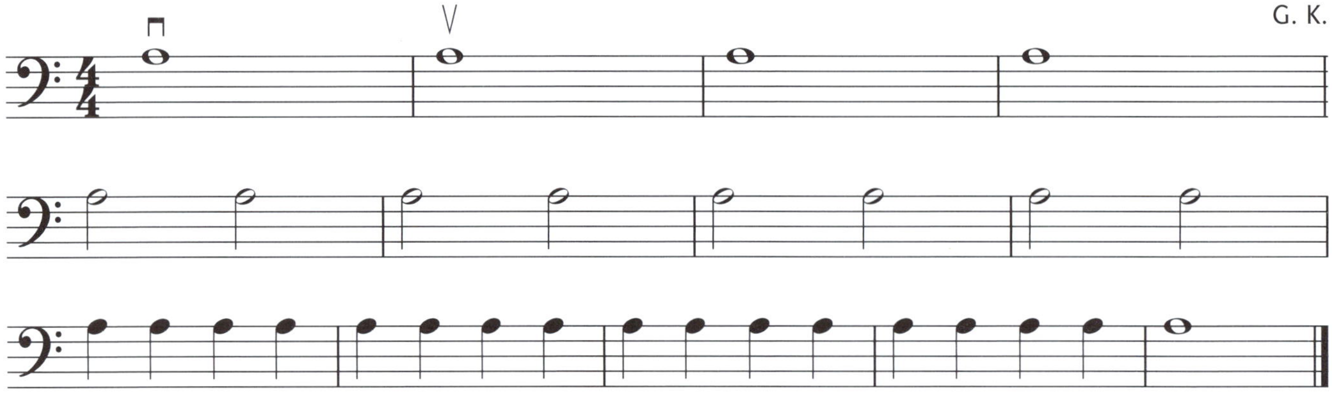

Accompaniment:
pizz. strumming

D 3rd cello part

Brackets are needed when a piece has repeats with different endings.

1. — 1: Play the measures (bars) under this bracket the first time, then repeat.

2. — 2: Second time, skip the first bracket and go straight to the second bracket.

Track 4

Little March

G. K.

Quarter rest (crotchet rest) 𝄽 = 1 beat

Write a little piece for open strings:

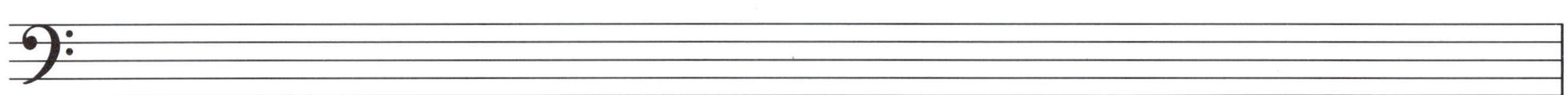

Exercises

Write in the note names:

Write whole notes (semibreves) on the right lines:

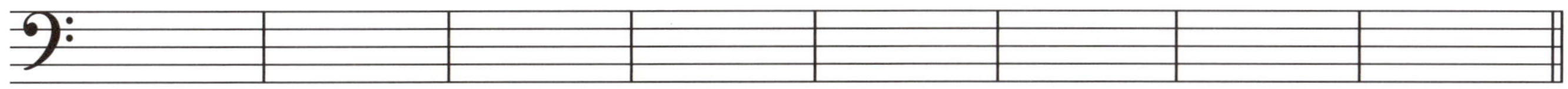

Different note values need different amounts of bow.
Pay attention to which part of the bow you have to use:

WB	=	Whole bow
UH	=	Upper half
LH	=	Lower half

↺ = „Travelling trough space“
Carry the bow through the air back to the frog.

Counting like a Maybug

Exercises with different note values

1.

2.

Oh dear! I've left out a few notes here: can you write them in?

3.

Oh no! The bar lines are missing here: please write them in now.

4.

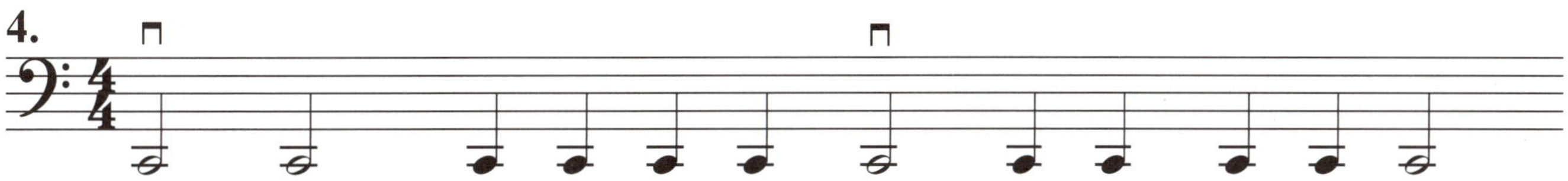

Track 5 Jam track 1: Let's put a piece together

1. Play each 'section of the puzzle' along with the recording for a while.
2. Alternate freely between sections.
3. Try playing from memory.
4. Write out your own rhythms below and give your piece a name. If you copy this page (several times), you can cut out the sections and stick them onto a piece of paper in any order you choose.

Name of the piece ______________________ Composer ______________________

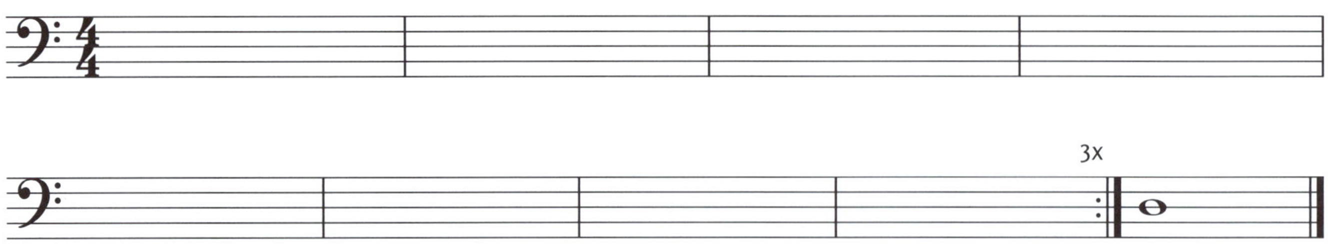

Accompaniment:

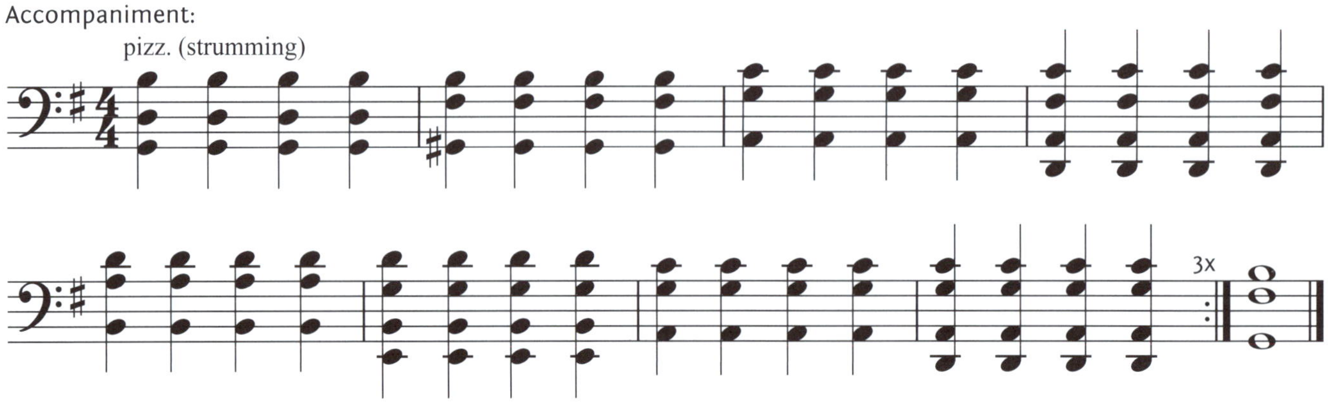

String crossing

Pluck all the pieces first, then use the bow!

Track 6/7 **Skip To My Lou**

Traditional
Arr.: Gabriel Koeppen

on G and D strings

Track 8/9 **Lullaby**

G. K.

On D and A strings

Track 10/11

Tom Dooley

Traditional
Arr.: Gabriel Koeppen

Exercises with string crossing

1.

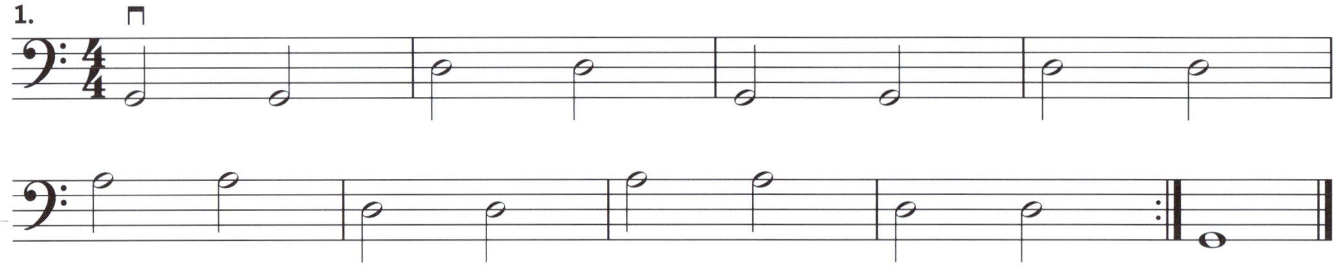

2.

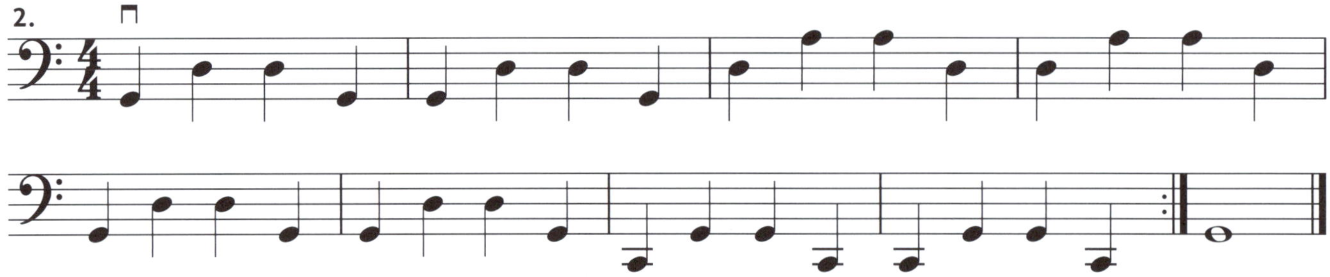

3.

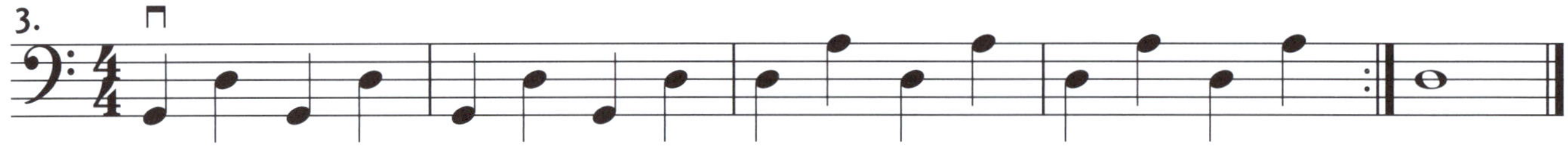

4.

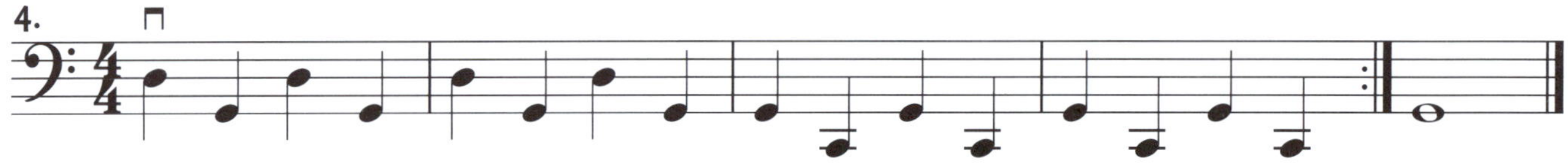

Write a piece of your own for open strings using various note values:

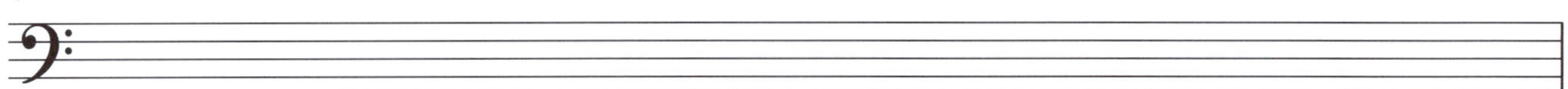

Tune book p. 4

Playing with the left hand

This is how to place your fingers

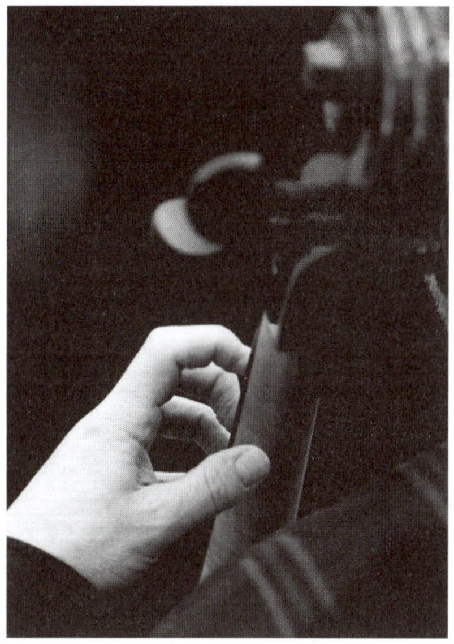

The thumb rests opposite the middle finger

Preliminary exercises

Shape your left hand into a telescope and look through: now your fingers are nicely curled. Now place your index and middle fingers on the A string. The thumb rests on the other side of the neck. Forearm and hand make a straight line (don't bend the wrist). For the following exercises it doesn't matter what point you press on the string.

Exercise 1: press the A string onto the fingerboard for a few seconds and let go again. Repeat several times.

Exercise 2: Try plucking the A string while pressing down. If the note sounds dull and fuzzy, you need to press harder.

Exercise 3: Press lightly on the string and slide merrily up and down the string. How do the notes change as you change the fingering position?

Exercise 4: knock your fingers hard against the string.

Try these exercises on the other strings. Can you play without looking at your fingers?

Fingering

The fingers on the left hand are given numbers. Numbers above musical notation (called 'fingering') help you to use the correct finger.

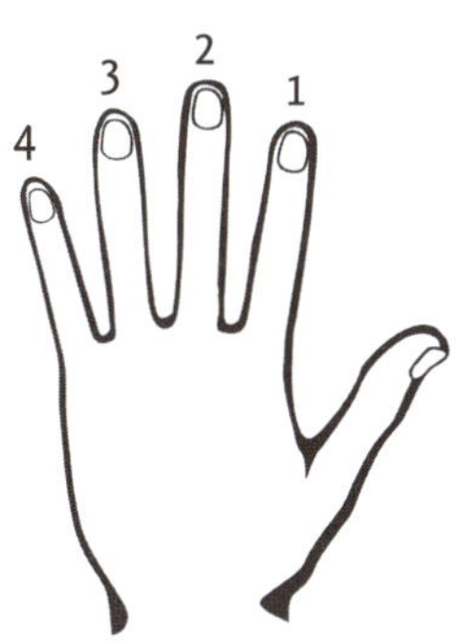

4 = little finger
3 = ring finger
2 = middle finger
1 = index finger

Now use your 2nd finger to play the cuckoo's call on the D string.
Pluck and then play with the bow.

2 0
Cuck - oo

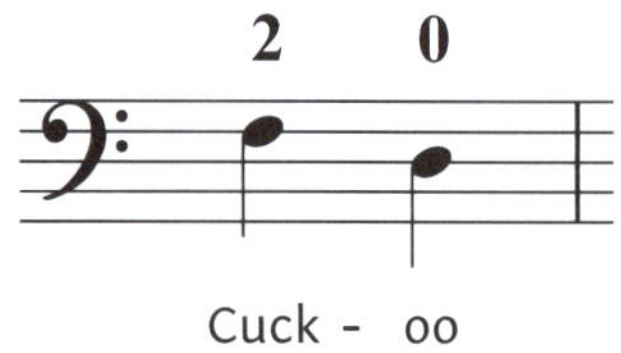

Now you can play the beginning of the cuckoo's song with your teacher:

2nd finger on the D string

If you play with your 2nd finger on the D string, the note F will sound.
Always place your 1st finger at the same time, leaving the thumb on the neck.

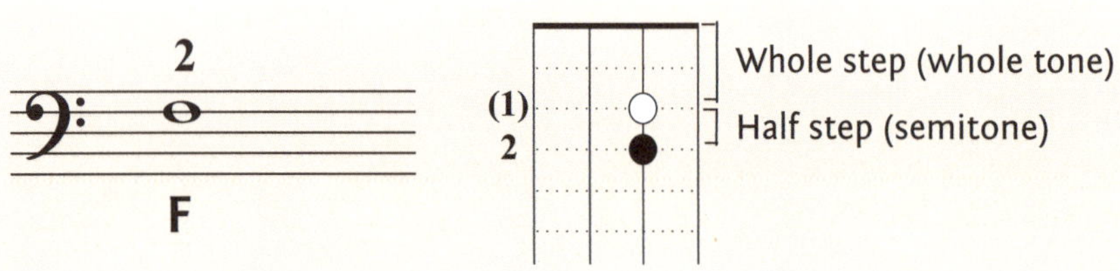

Exercise

Track 12/13 First Rock

Powerfully

G. K.

Track 14/15 Waiting

G. K.

Repeat ad lib.

Tune book p. 5

1st finger on the D string

If you place your first finger on the D string you can play an E.

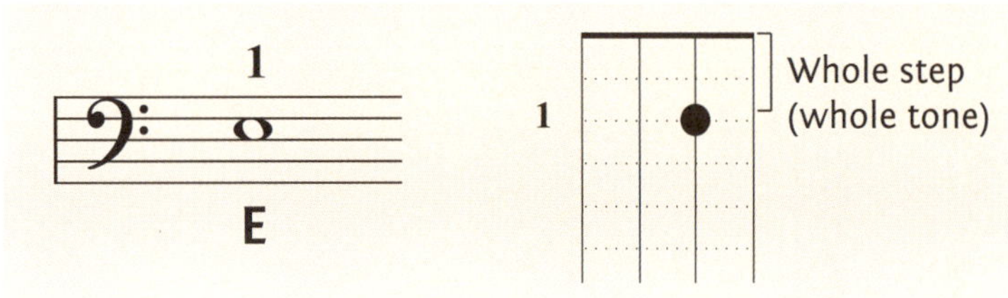

Exercise

Track 16/17 Rain Song

Sadly

G. K.

Make up a little piece using E and D:

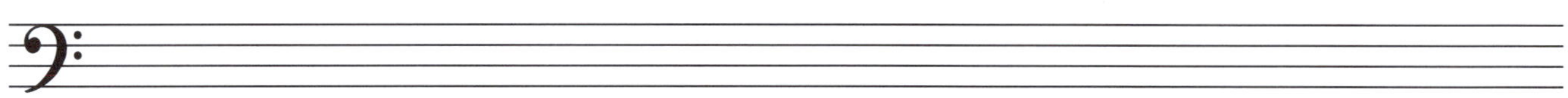

Track 18/19 Don't Tell Me Lies

Half rest (minim rest) ▬ = 2 beats

G. K.

*) stamp your foot

Tune book p. 6

Track 20 Playing by Ear

Now I'll play you five sequences of notes on the D string on the recording, just playing the open string and first finger. Make sure you always count to the end of each measure (bar)! You can write out your part, too.

Your teacher can give you more aural tests in lessons

1st and 2nd fingers on the D string

Ballad

G. K.

Track 21/22 Catch me if you can

G. K.

Make up a little piece using D, E and F:

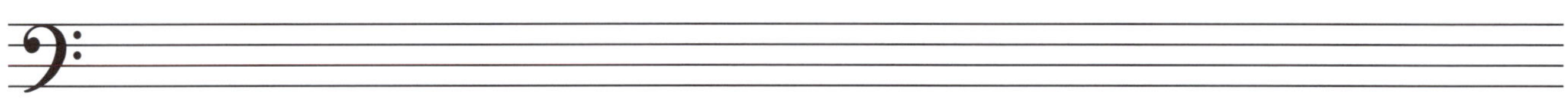

Easy Blues

G. K.

3rd cello part

Track 23/24

In the Desert

G. K.

Repeat ad lib.

Piano part

4th finger on the D string

Repeat finger exercises 1 and 2 on page 19. Place all your fingers on the fingerboard.
When you play the 4th finger on the D string the note G will sound. Put all your fingers down at once:

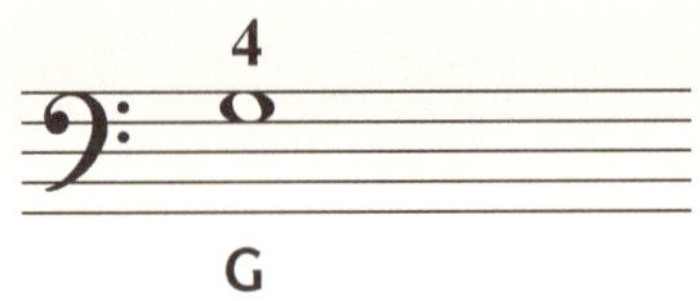

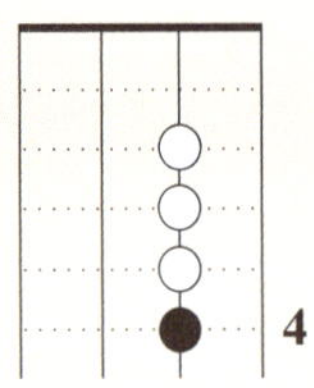

Find the notes:

High and low G sound good together

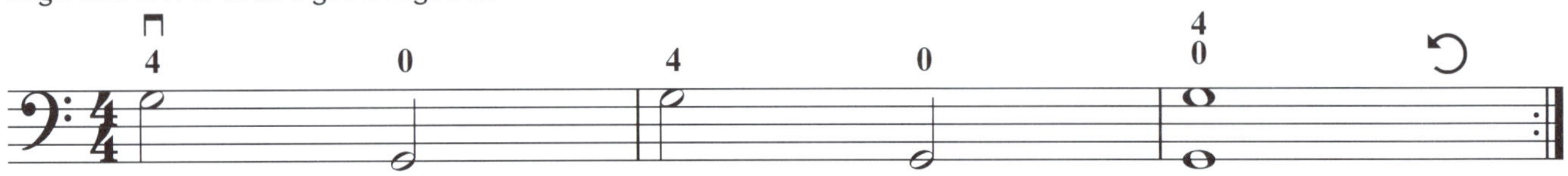

Just one note

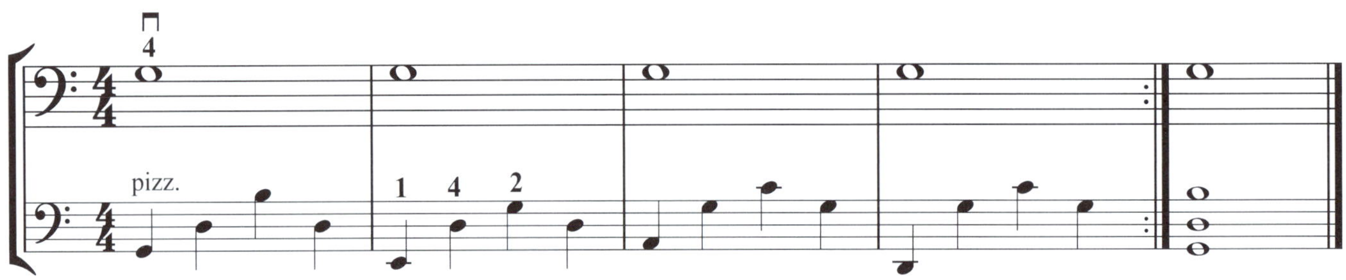

Track 25/26 Robot

Leave 4th finger in place

G. K.

Tune book p. 7-8

Four notes on the D string

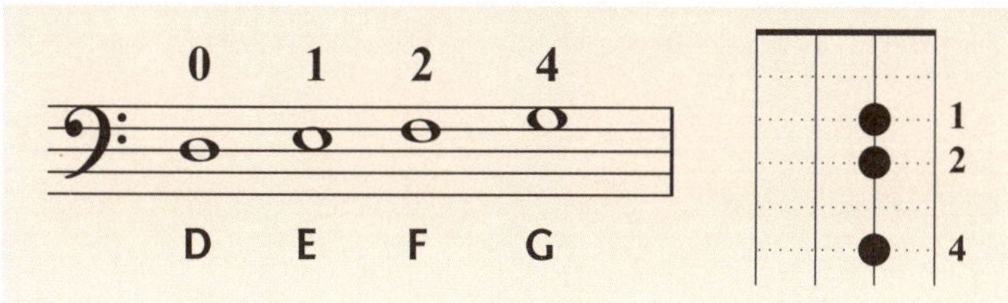

Get your fingers ready

Track 27/28 Party time

G. K.

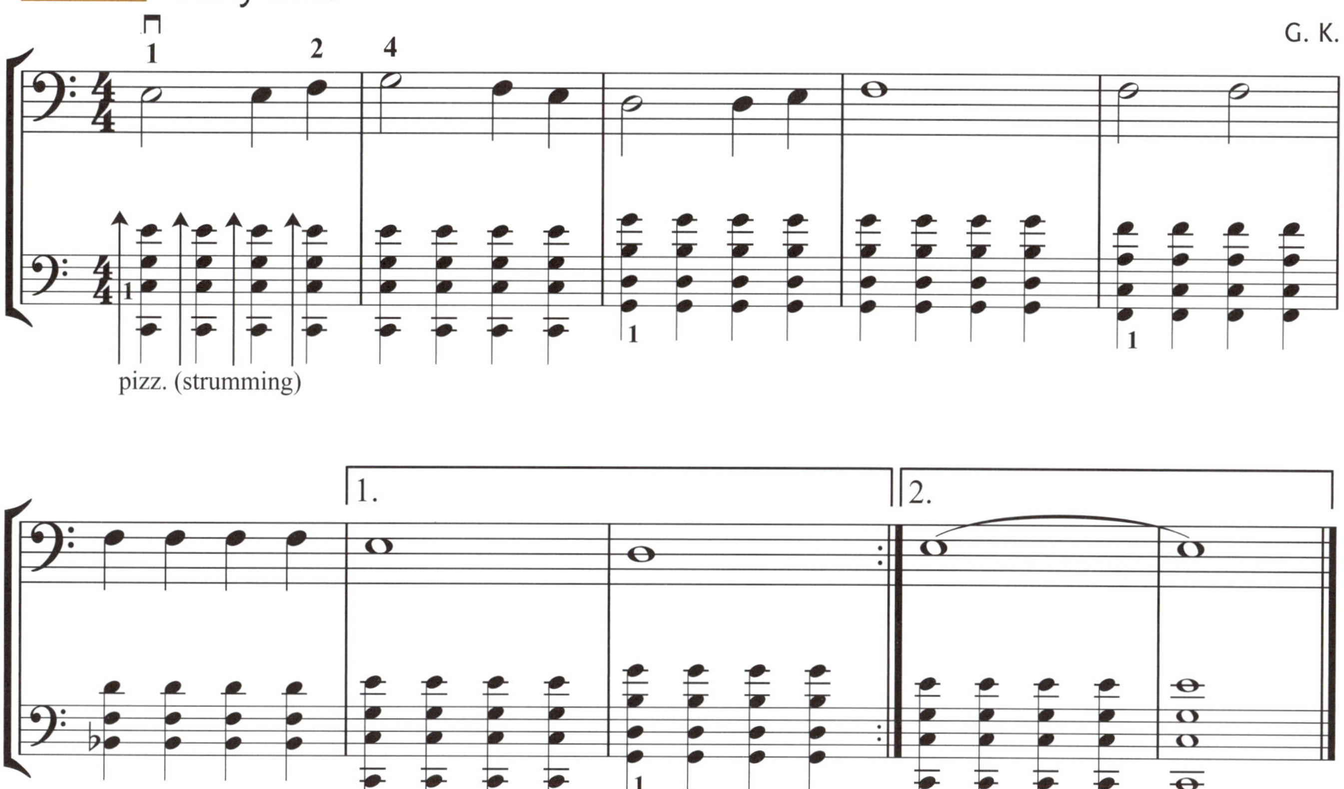

D 3rd cello part

Hungarian Canon

Traditional

(end of the canon)

> = accent (strong emphasis)

Track 29/30

Keep Going

G. K.

Exercises

Write in the note names:

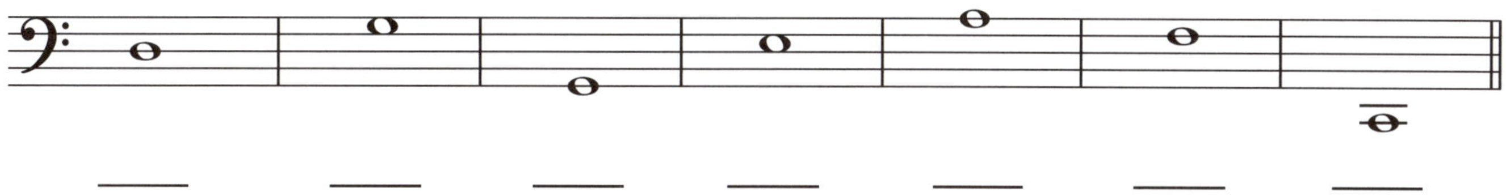

Write whole notes (semibreves) on the right lines (only write notes on the D string):

Guess the notes

Shut your eyes. Your teacher will play the open D string and another note on the same string. Try to play the same sequence of notes. After a while, swap: now you can test your teacher. You could keep score to see who gets it right most often!

Do you know what these intervals are called?

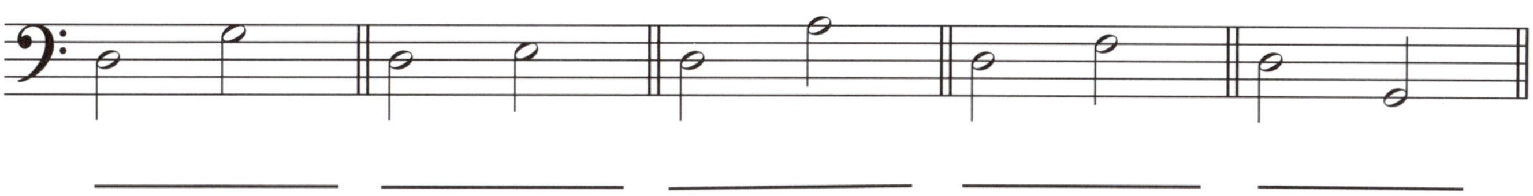

Ideas for other aural tests or a little piece:

Four notes on the A string

Get your fingers ready

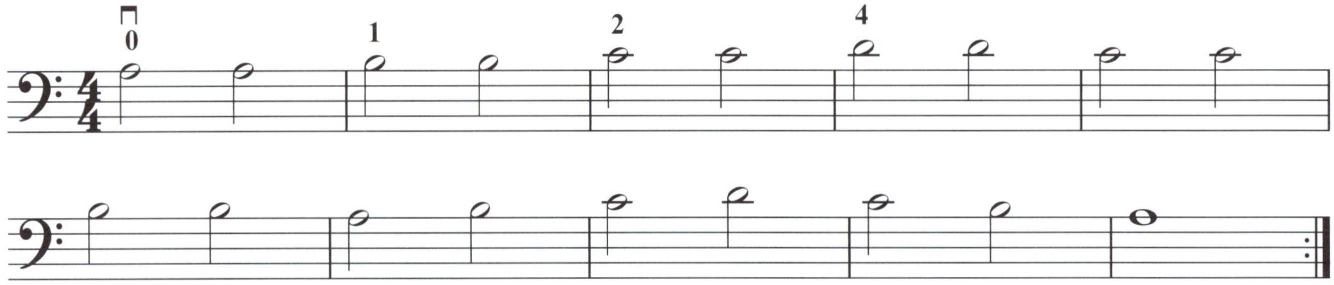

Track 31/32 **Consolation**

G. K.

This piece begins with an upbeat: this is an incomplete measure (bar) at the beginning of a piece. The upbeat is usually played unaccented. The upbeat and final measure (bar) added together make a complete measure (bar).

Track 33/34 **Dance of the Vikings**

Powerfully

G. K.

Repeat ad lib.

T Tune book p. 10

D Piano part

Write in the note names:

Write whole notes (semibreves) on the right lines (only write notes on the A string):

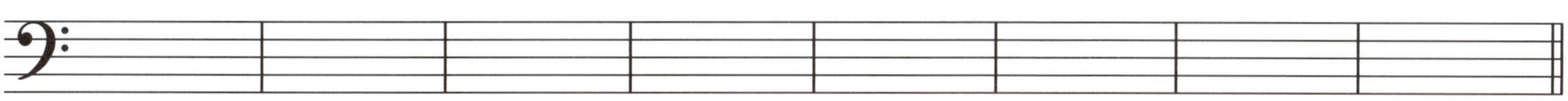

B A C D A B A C

'Guess the notes' again

1. as on p. 29, with notes on the A string
2. with other combinations of notes

Track 35

Jam track 2: Rocking Strings

Anyone learning to juggle starts off with just two balls. In the following piece we'll try juggling with notes. You can't go wrong, just alternate between C and A as you please. Listen to the rhythm of the accompaniment (on the recording or by your teacher) and accent the first beat of each measure (bar). If you don't know what to play next, put in a rest or stay on the same note. When you've tried it out a bit, write down your ideas – and your composition is done!

Carry on playing freely using A and C

Compose a piece with these notes and play it along with the jam track.

Name of the piece

Composer

Accompaniment:

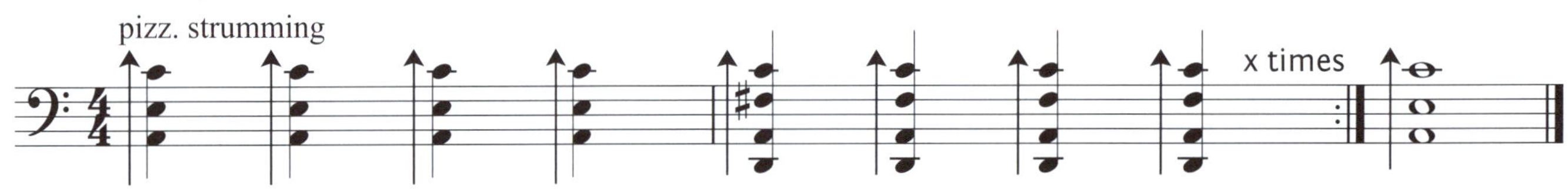

Playing on A and D Strings

Little Duet

Arr.: Gabriel Koeppen

Go Tell Aunt Nancy

Arr.: Gabriel Koeppen

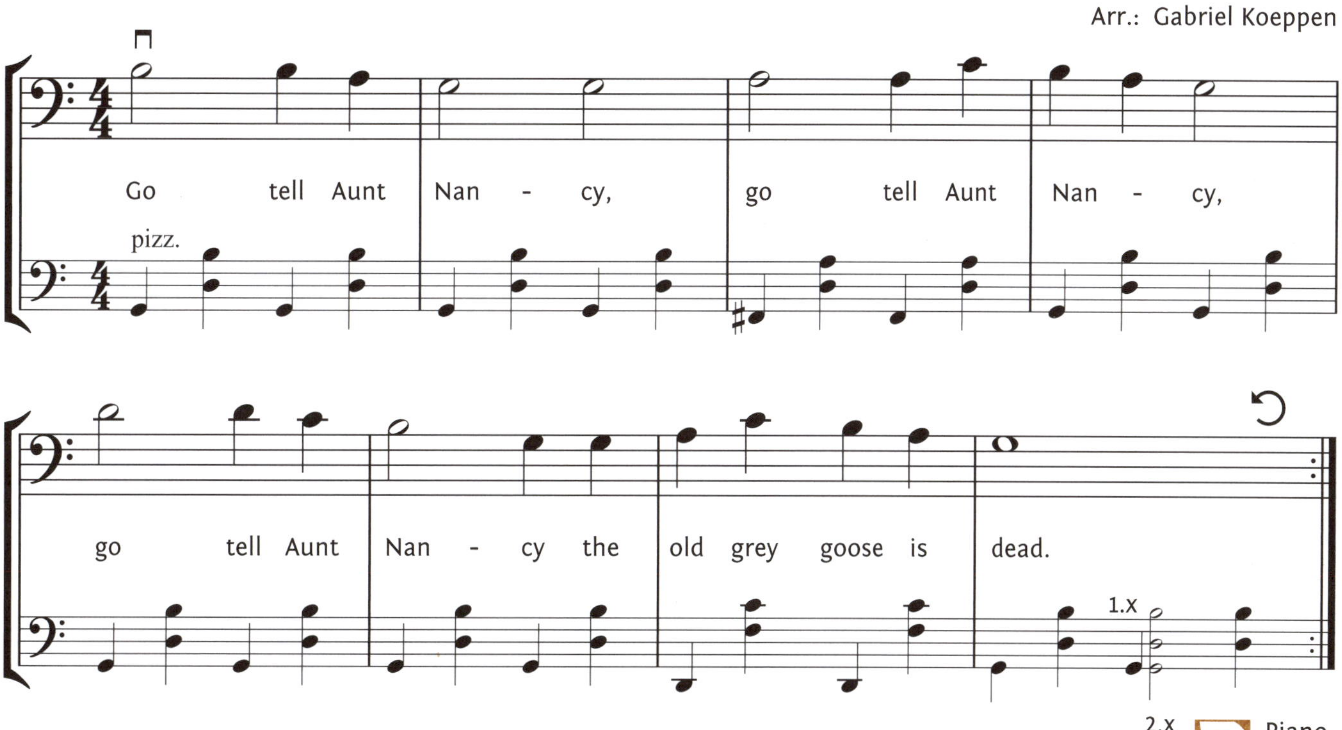

Piano part

Track 36/37 **Lucky Fellow**

G. K.

Playing on the G String

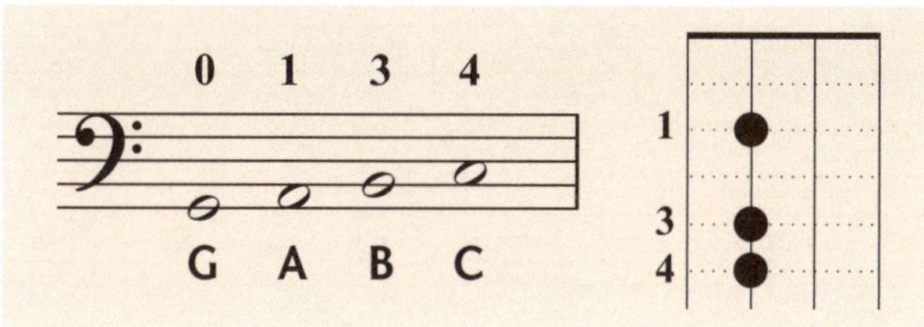

Get your fingers ready

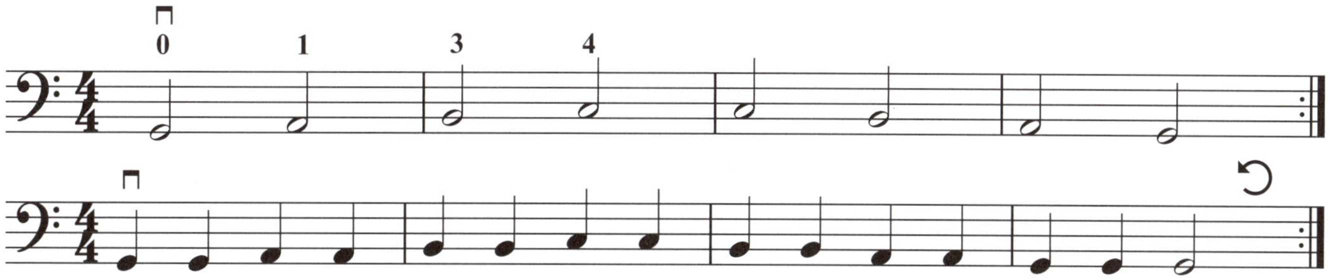

There's a Man Fallen in the Well

Merrily We Roll Along

Traditional
Arr.: Gabriel Koeppen

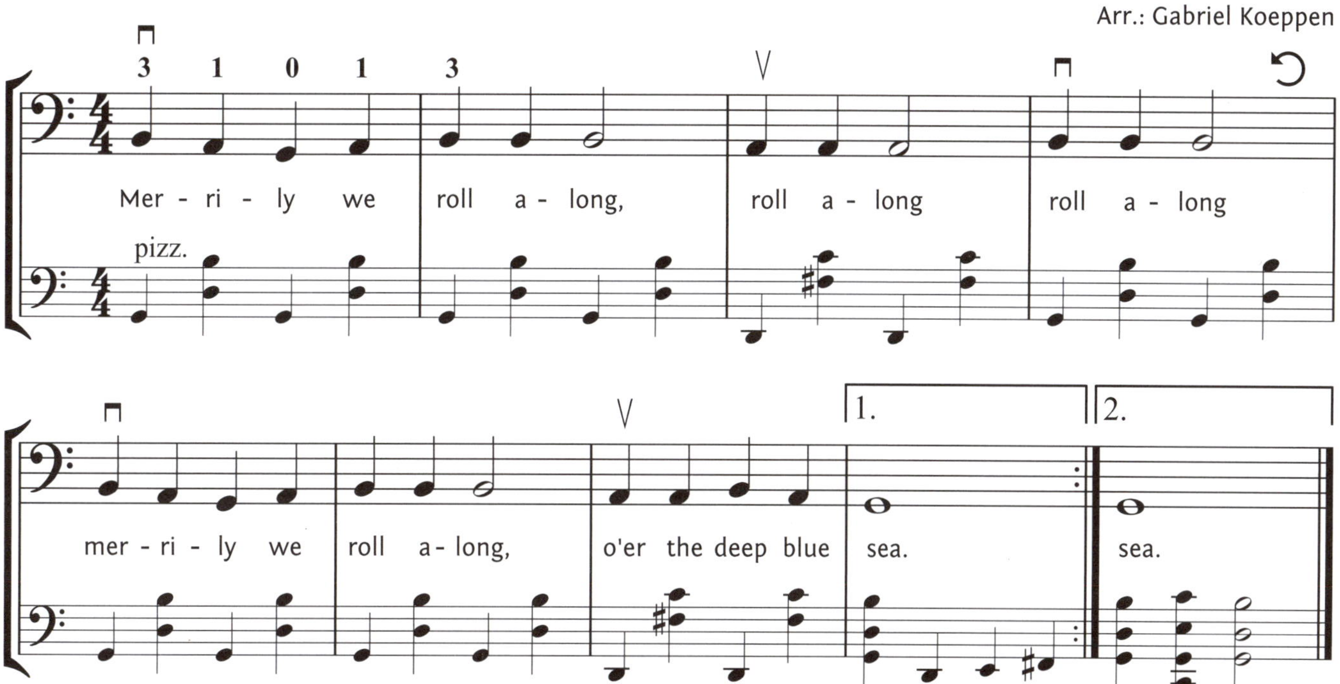

Can you play this tune from memory, too?

D Piano part

Little Study

G. K.

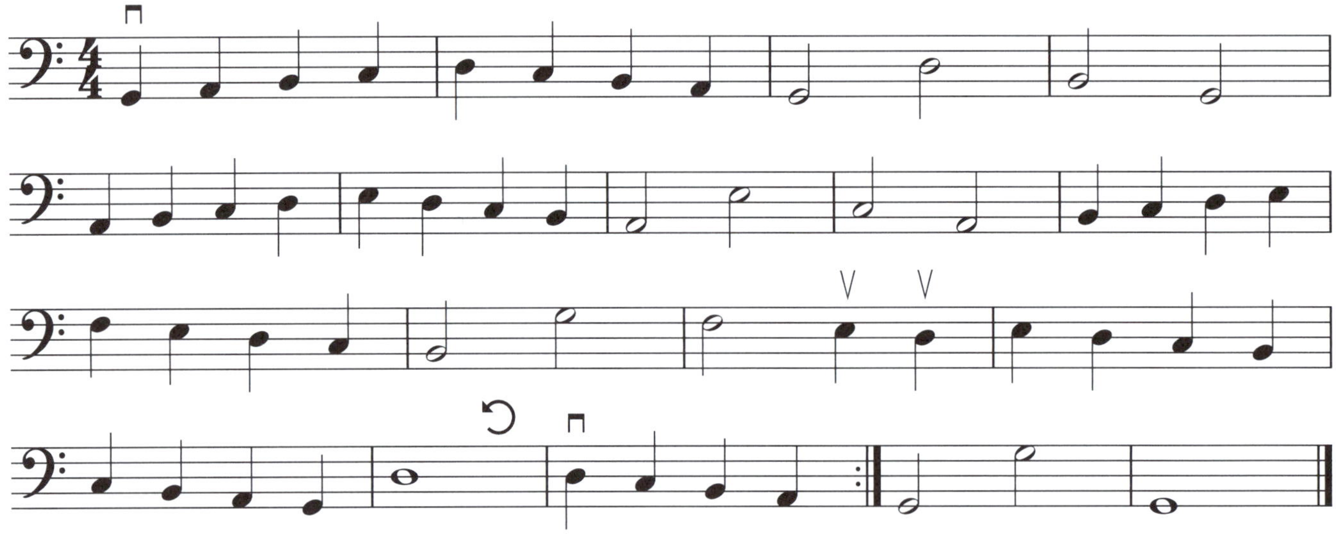

Tune book p. 14

Dynamics (volume)

You can make a piece sound more interesting by varying the volume. In musical notation we use a few abbreviations:

f = forte (strong, loud)
mf = mezzoforte (moderately loud)
p = piano (soft)

Echo Game

Your teacher plays two measures (bars), you play an 'echo' (*p*). Then swap over.
Can you imitate a pattern without reading the music?

Invent other echo calls, perhaps using words.
Can you write them down? Try swapping parts, too.

Turn back a few pages, work out dynamics for your favourite pieces and write them in.

Track 38/39 **Swanee River**

Traditional
Arr.: Gabriel Koeppen

D Piano part

Exercises

Write in the note names:

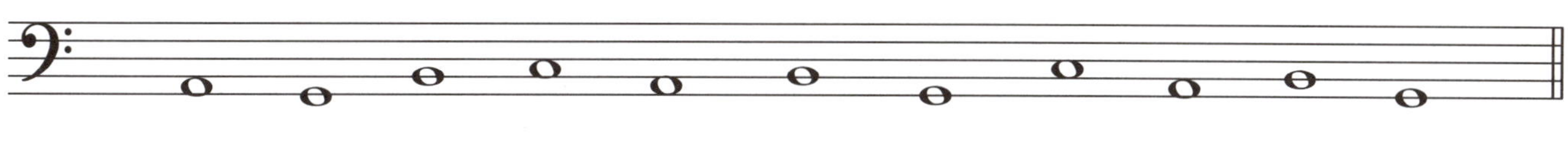

Write whole notes (semibreves) on the right lines (only writing notes on the G string):

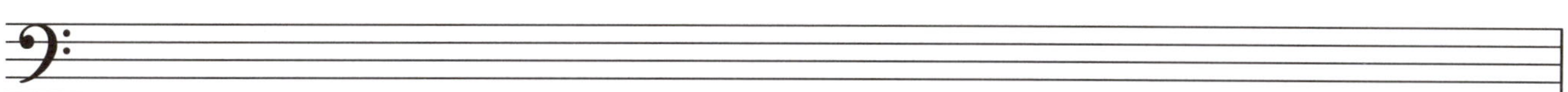

A G B C G A B G C A B G

Playing on the C String

Get your fingers ready

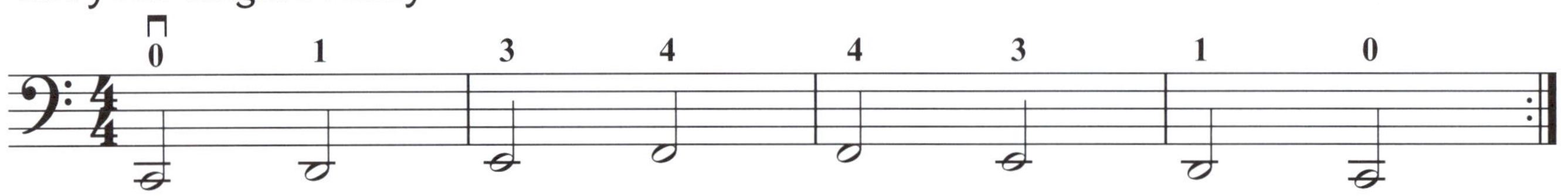

There's a Man Fallen in the Well

Carry on playing from memory and write out the rest of the song

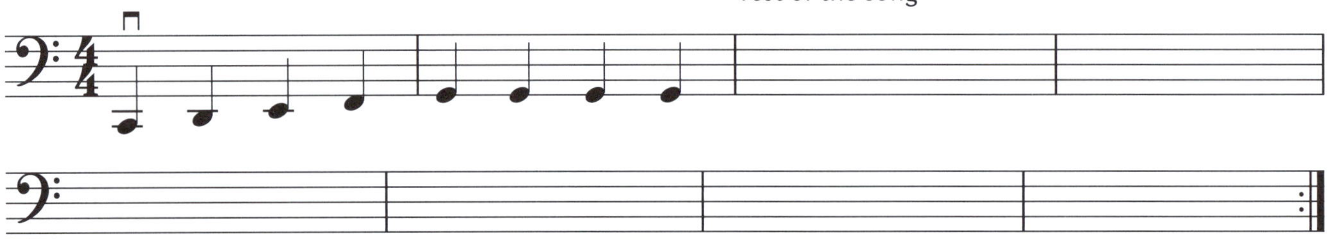

Swingin' The Bass

pizz. or arco

G. K.

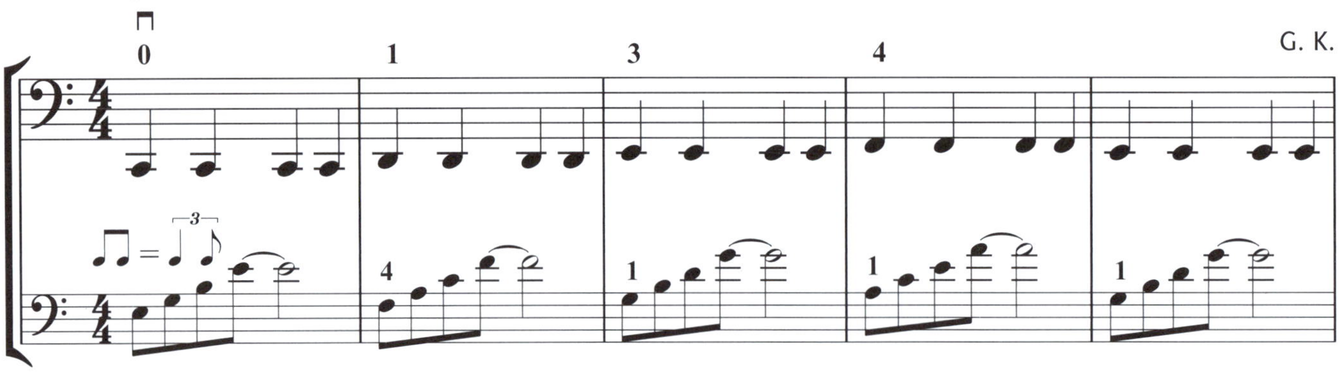

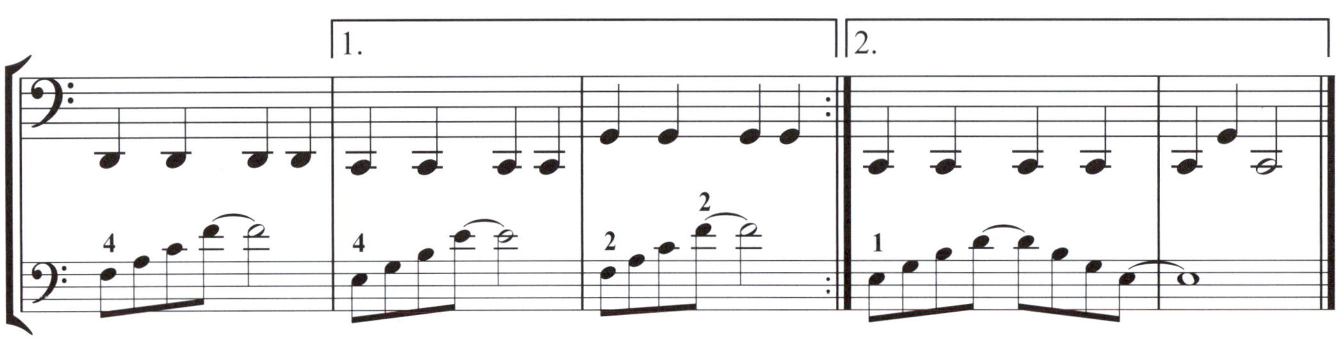

D Piano part

The Little Tuba Player

G. K.

From: G. Koeppen, Nette Duette (Duets for Fun), Schott ED 21395

D Piano part

Exercises

Write in the note names:

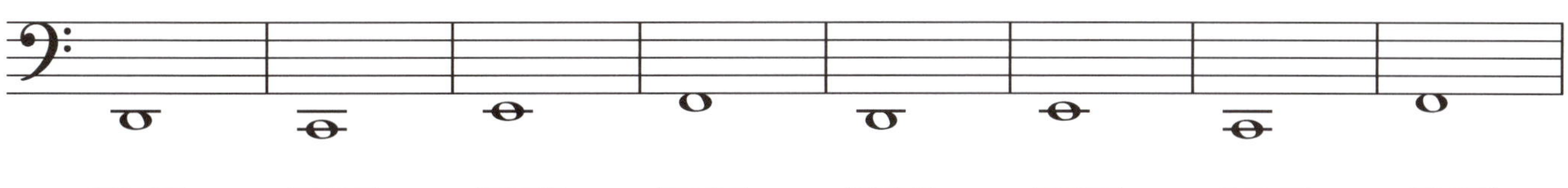

Write whole notes (semibreves) on the right lines (only writing notes on the C string):

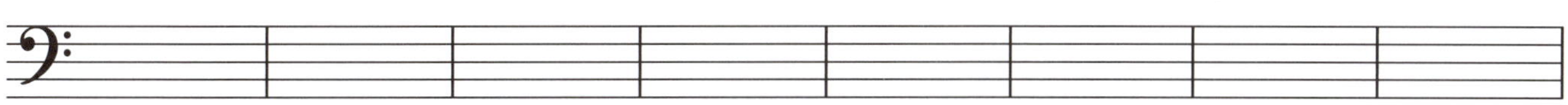

D C E F C D C E

C major scale

C major broken chord

Track 40/41 The Fat Hippopotamus

Heavily

G. K.

Now try playing 'Swanee River' on the C string. Start on E (3rd finger).

D Piano part

Eighth notes (quavers)

A eighth note (quaver) sounds half as long as a quarter note (crotchet): ♩ = ♫
So if you count in quarter note (crotchet) beats, each beat will have two eighth notes (quavers.)
Single eighth notes (quavers) have a flag: ♪
Groups of eithth notes (quavers) are joined with a beam, e.g. ♫ or ♫♫

For eighth notes (quavers) you only need to use half as much bow as for quarter notes (crotchets).

Exercises with eight notes (quavers)

Write a piece using eight notes (quavers) and other note values:

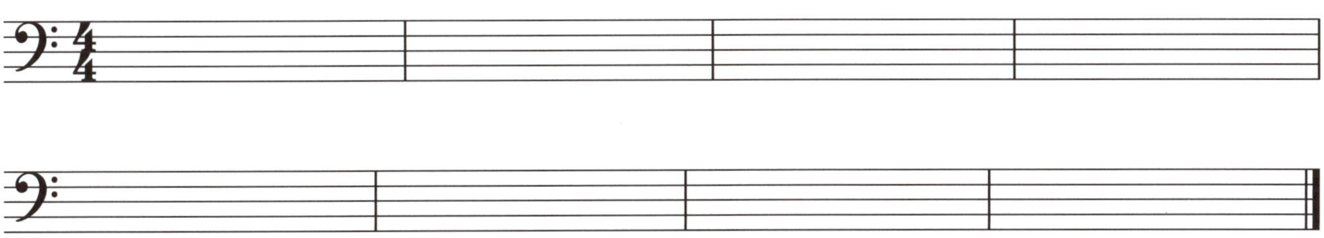

Track 42/43 Eighths Boogie

G. K.

What Shall We Do

Shanty
Arr.: Gabriel Koeppen

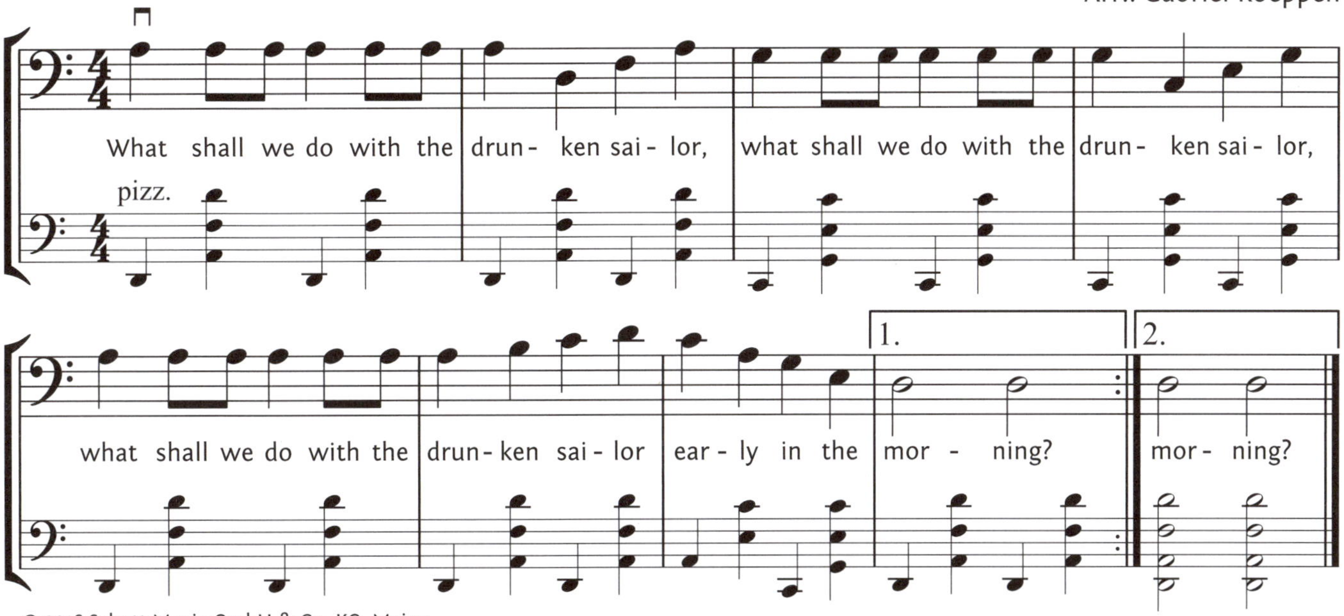

D Piano part

i A dot after a note lengthens it by half its value: 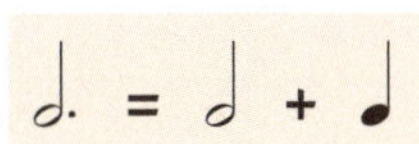

Track 44/45

Old MacDonald

Traditional
Arr.: Gabriel Koeppen

T Tune book p. 16

D Piano part

Writing a little tune

Try writing a piece with eight notes (quavers) and other note values too (and rests, of course). It doesn't matter if you can't think of anything straight away. Sometimes an idea comes when you speak some words: this might be a poem, for example, or any kind of nonsense such as the words that follow.
Where are the accents? Which syllables should sound longer and which are shorter? You can jot down a rhythm on one line and then write a tune on the stave with the same rhythm.

Keep to just a few notes at first

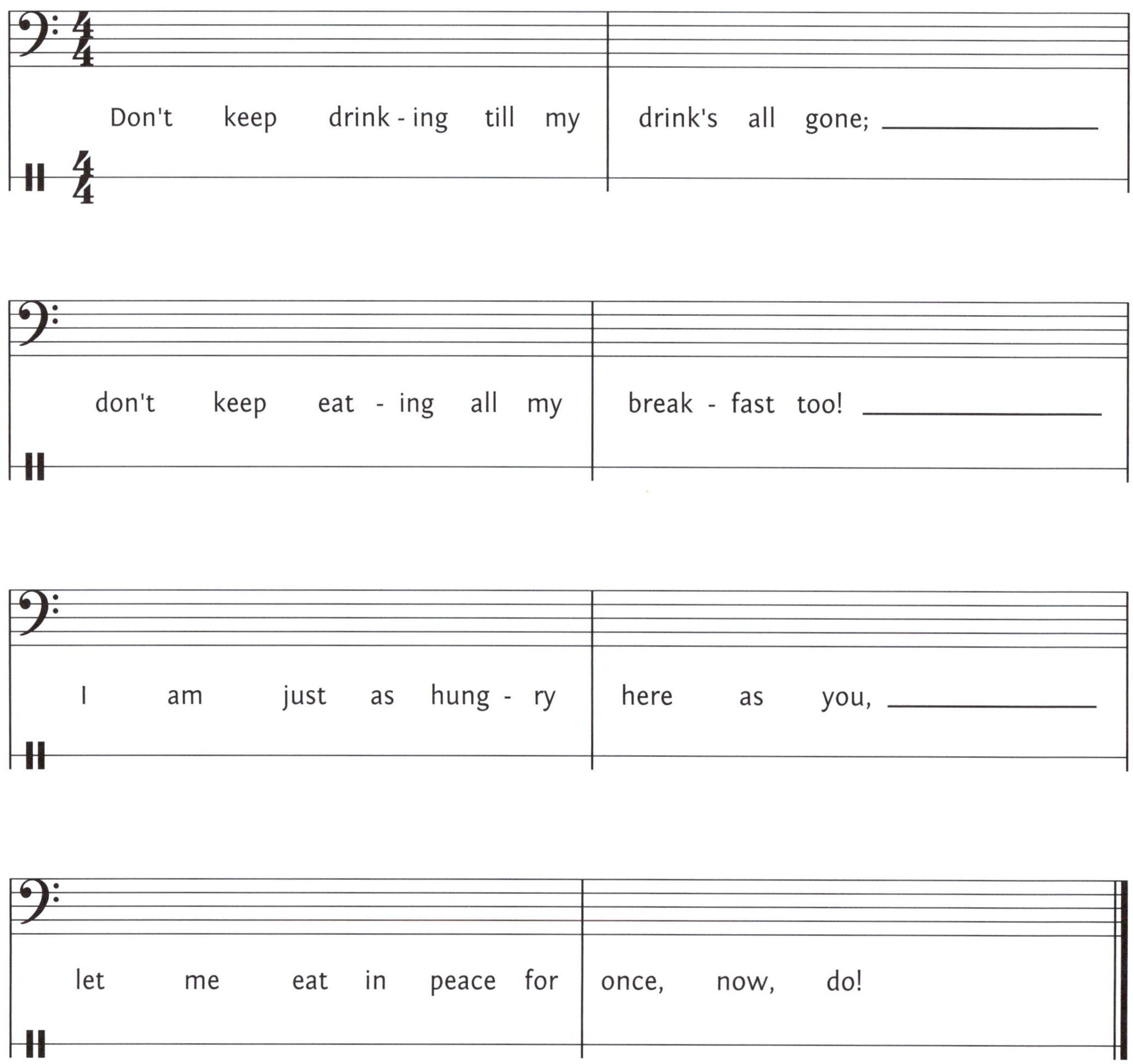

Now write your own words, songs and pieces – and make your fortune!

Accidentals

♯ A sharp ♯ raises the next note by a half step (semitone): F becomes F♯.
Just play with the next finger up, in this case with the 3rd finger instead of the 2nd finger. An accidental lasts for a whole measure (bar), until the next bar line.

3rd finger on the D string

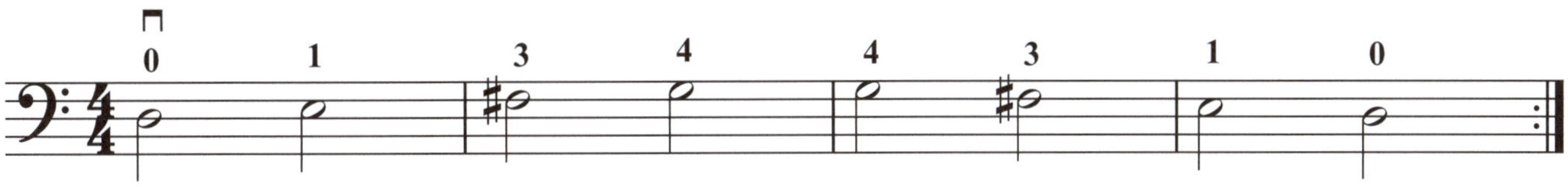

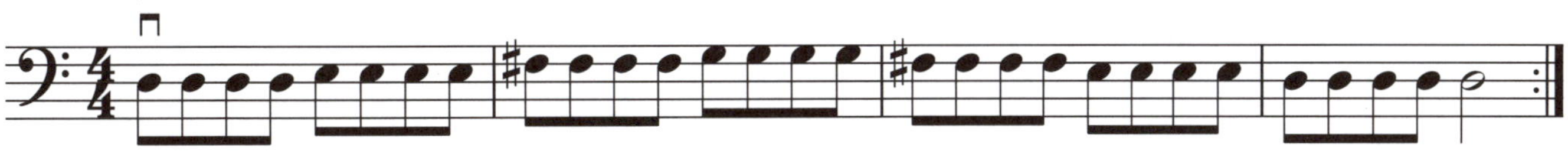

G major scale

G major broken chord

Merrily We Roll Along

Keep on playing from memory and write out the rest of the song.

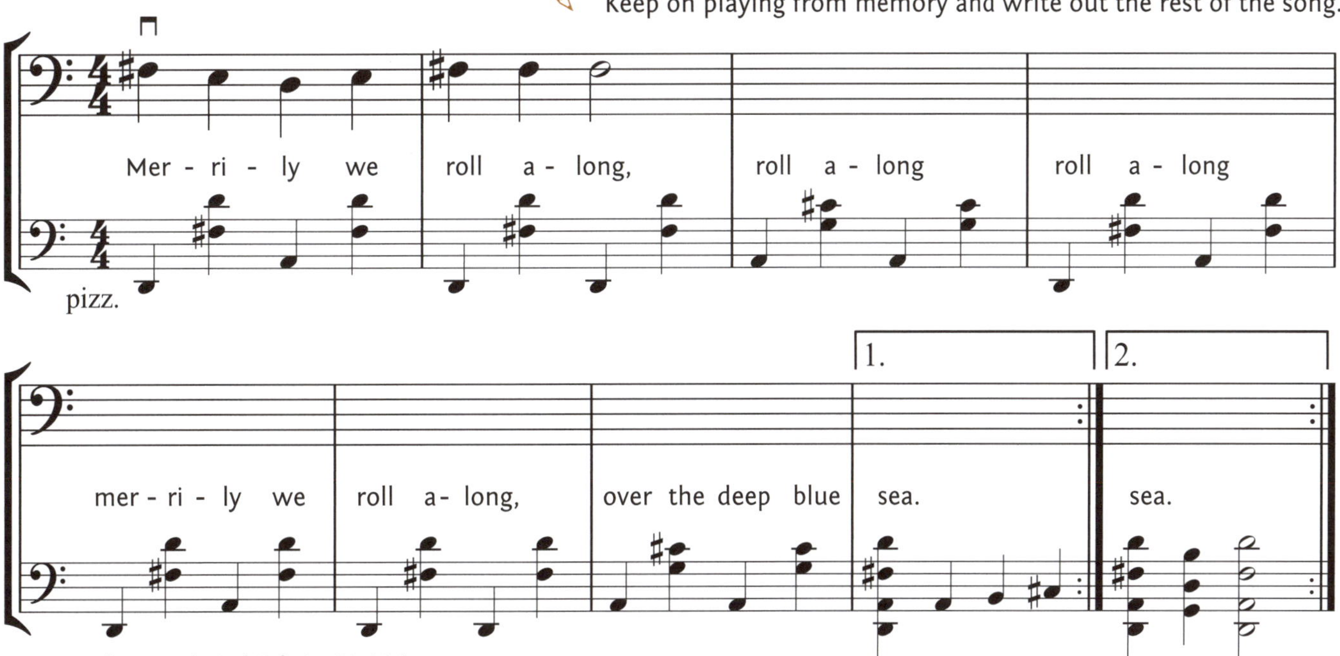

If a key signature is given at the beginning of the stave, it applies to the whole piece!

Fermata 𝄐
the note is held on longer than the printed value.

Track 46/47 Missing You

G. K.

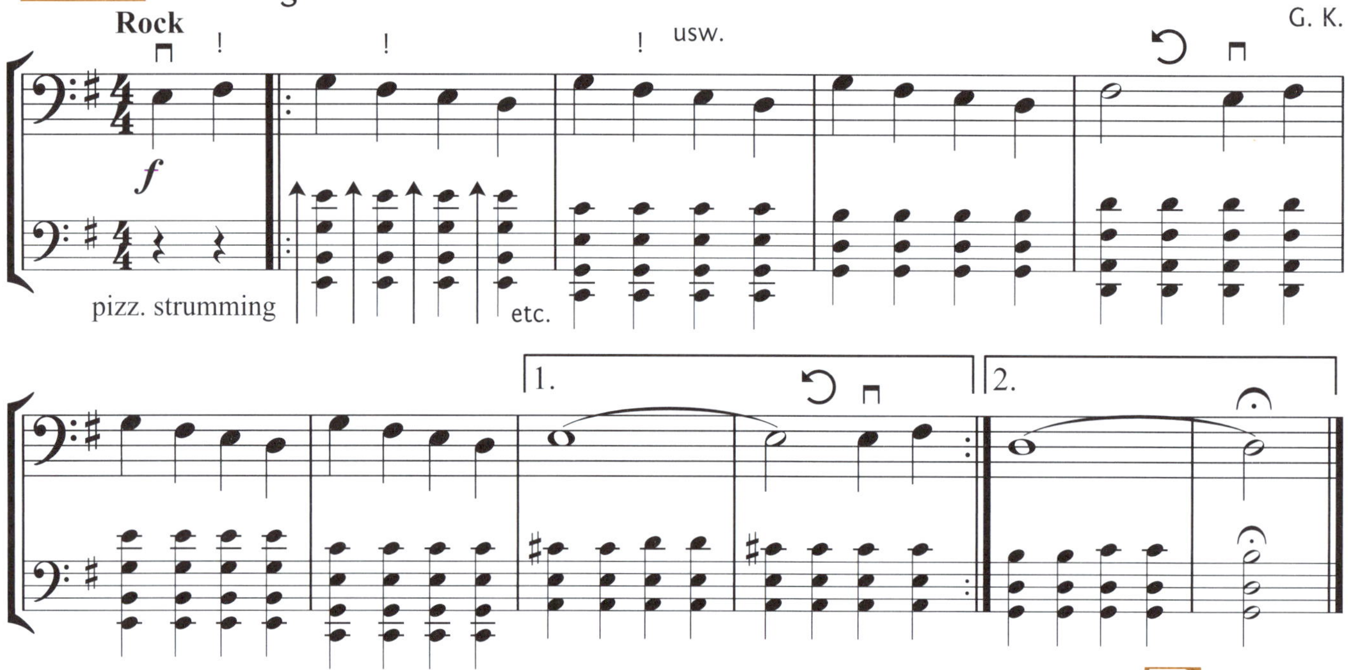

Piano part

Jesters' Dance

Anonymous 16th Century
Arr.: Gabriel Koeppen

Piano part

Track 48 **Jam Track 3: Ballad**

For example:

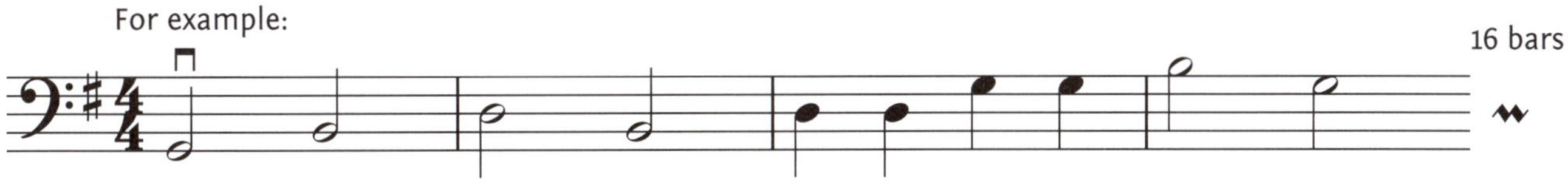

Keep on playing with the notes in the G major broken chord:

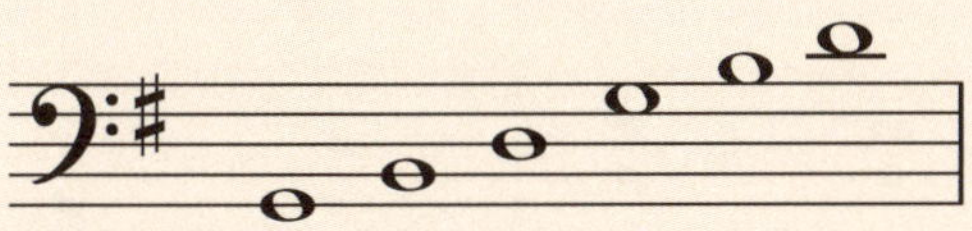

It's easier if you repeat notes

Write a piece of your own and play along with the jam track:

Name of the piece ____________________

Composer ____________________

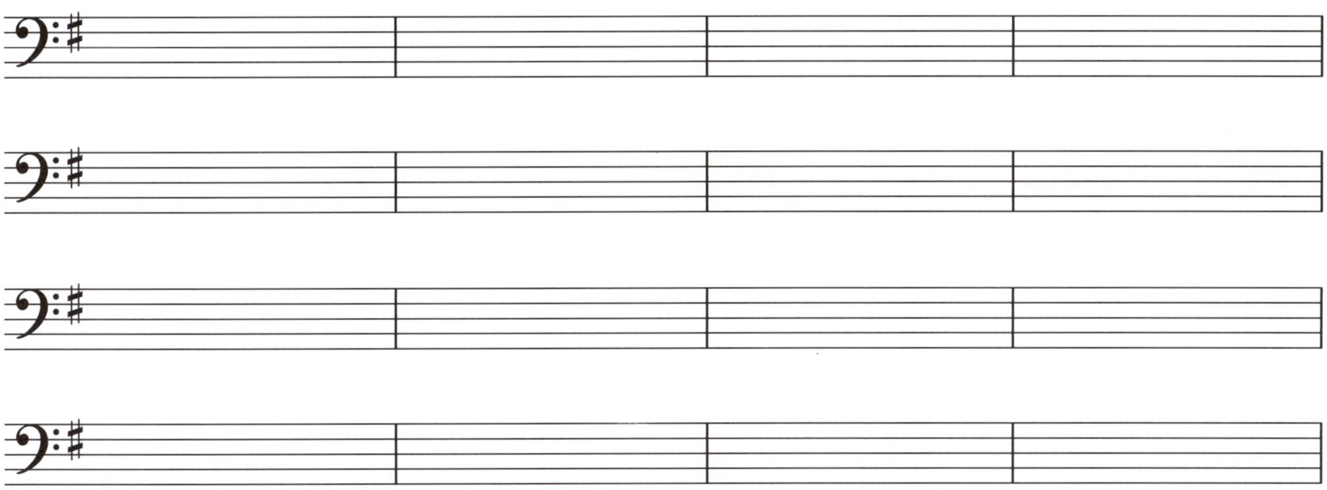

Accompaniment:
pizz. or arco

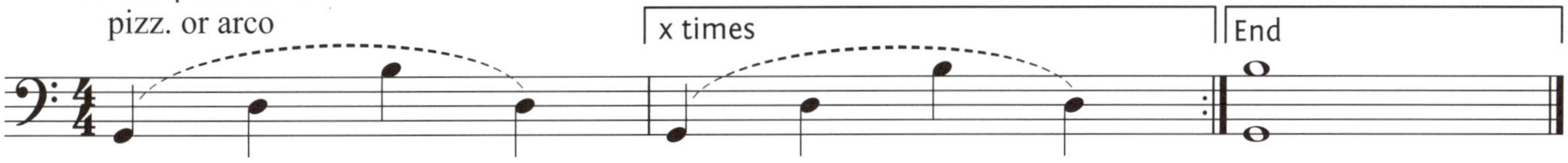

Hey, ho, hitch the cart up now

Canon in three parts
English translation:
Julia Rushworth

Track 49/50

Little Brown Jug

Traditional
Arr.: Gabriel Koeppen

Tune book p. 19

Piano part

3/4 time

The symbol $\frac{3}{4}$ at the beginning of the first line of music means the piece has three quarter note (crotchet) beats in each bar.
For example, a bar might have: ♩ ♩ ♩ | 𝅗𝅥. | 𝅗𝅥 ♩ |

Track 51 **Jam track 4: 3/4 Mish-mash**

Play each rhythm along with the recodring for a while.
Mix up the rhythms, play your own ideas along with the jam track and write a piece.

Name of the piece ______________________ Composer ______________________

Try playing the D on the A string, too.

Accompaniment:

Waltz: dance in 3/4 time

Waltz

G. K.

T Tune book p. 21

D Piano part

? Aural test

Your teacher will play you a short melody: is it in 3/4 or 4/4 time?
Now it's your turn: play your teacher the beginning of a tune you know.
You can play the tune on one note; what matters is to make the accents very clear.

Track 52/53 **Morning Has Broken**

Traditional
Arr.: G. Koeppen

ritardando (abbr. *rit.*) = getting slower

D Piano part

Fill in the rests:

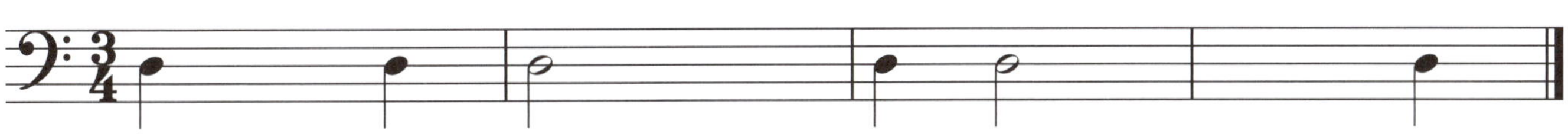

Write in bar lines:

Fill in the missing note values:

3rd finger on the A string

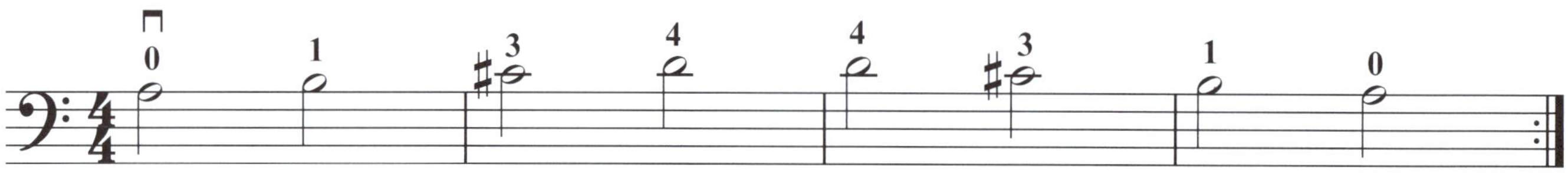

D major scale

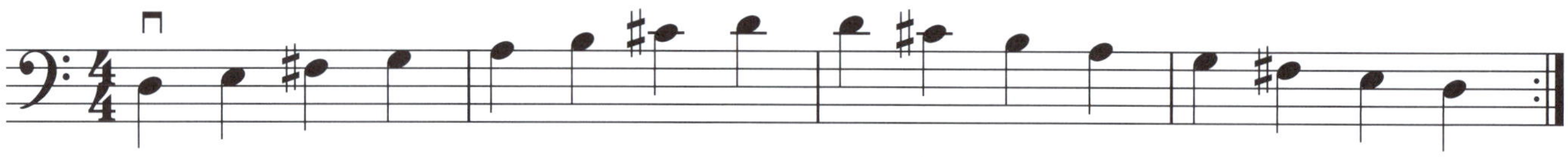

D major broken chord

Track 54/55 **Elegy**

In this piece the sharps appear in each measure (bar).

G. K.

L Later on, try playing legato, too

D Piano part

Track 56/57 **French Song**

From here on, key signatures appear at the beginning of each line of music.

Traditional

D Piano part

Track 58/59 **Allemande**

J. H. Schein (1586–1630)
Arr.: G. K.

T Tune book, p. 27

crescendo (cresc.) = getting louder

D Piano part

Legato

Legato means smooth and connected together. Notes linked with a slur are played 'in one bow': this means not changing bow between these notes.

Exercises: 2-note slurs

Apology

D Piano part

Exercises: 3-note slurs

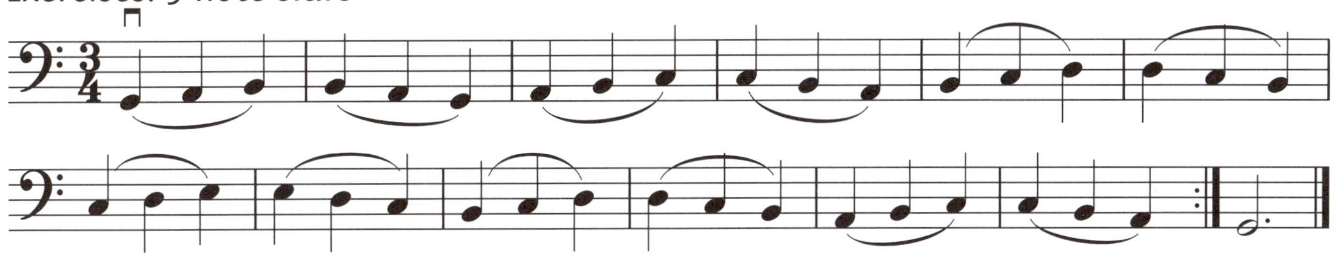

Track 60/61 **Vltava** (theme)

Bedřich Smetana
(1824–1884)
Arr.: G. Koeppen

Gavotte

from an old book of duets (1740)

Gavotte: Baroque dance in duple time, usually quite fast.

Exercises: 4-note slurs

Almond Blossom in China

Andante

G. K.

Track 62/63

Longing

Yearning

G. K.

Now have a go at working slurs into 'The Fat Hippopotamus' (p.40) and 'Elegy' (p. 52).

C major scale and broken chord

C major scale, two octaves

Here are a few bowing patterns. Further on in the book you'll find more.

etc.

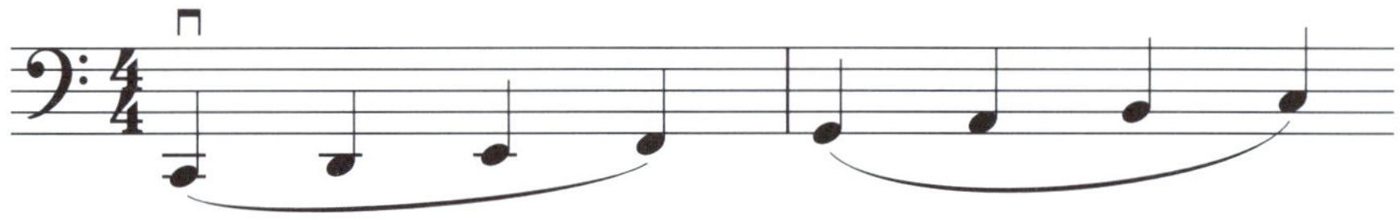

etc.

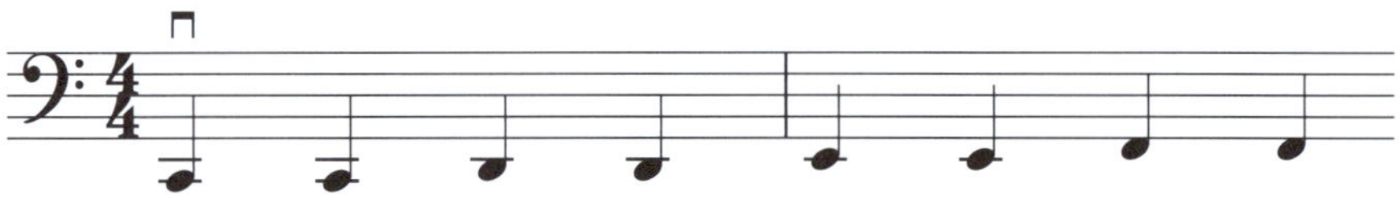

etc.

etc.

C major broken chord, two octaves

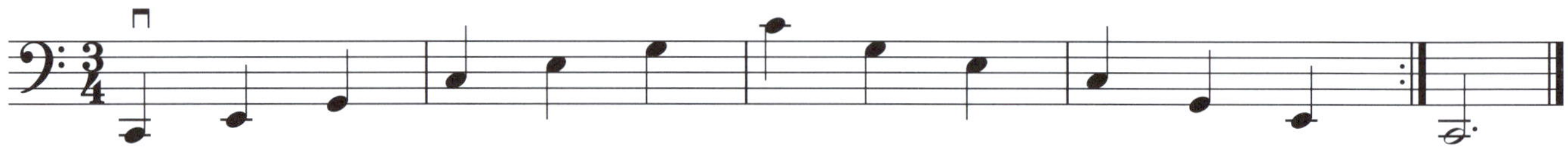

Bowing patterns:

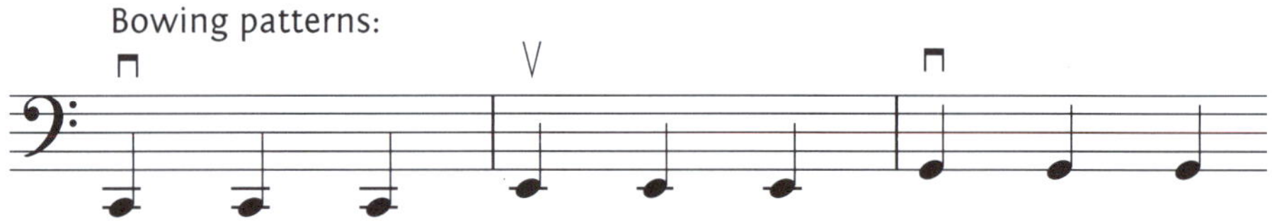

etc.

etc.

etc.

2nd finger on the G string

♭ The flat sign ♭ lowers the notes that follow by a half step (semitone). Just play with the next finger down, in this case the 2nd finger. The note B becomes B♭.

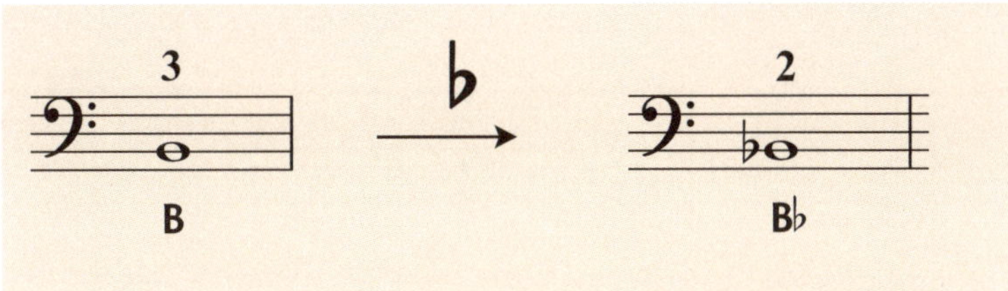

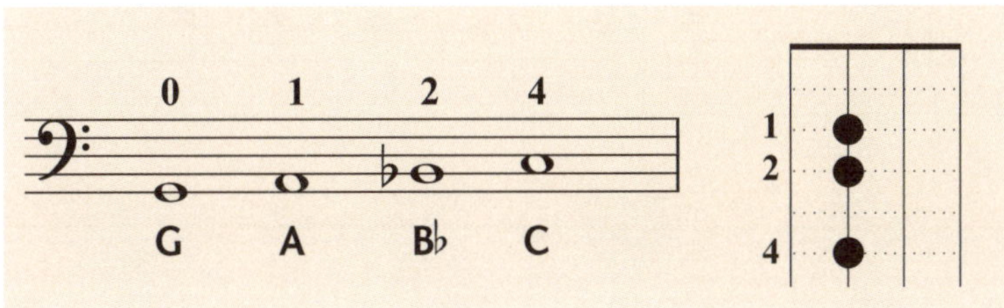

Going for a Walk

G. K.

Write a piece for 2nd finger on the G string:

When two notes appear above one another, play both strings at the same time (double stopping).

Aimless Tootling

G. K.

Track 64/65

Rainy City Blues

Slowly

G. K.

ritardando (abbr. *rit.*) = getting slower

A natural sign cancels a sharp or flat, just in that measure (bar).

Echo Minuet

Arr.: Erich Doflein

Vivace

2nd finger on the C string

The accidental ♭ before the E lowers it by a half step (semitone) to E♭.
Play with 2nd finger instead of 3rd finger.

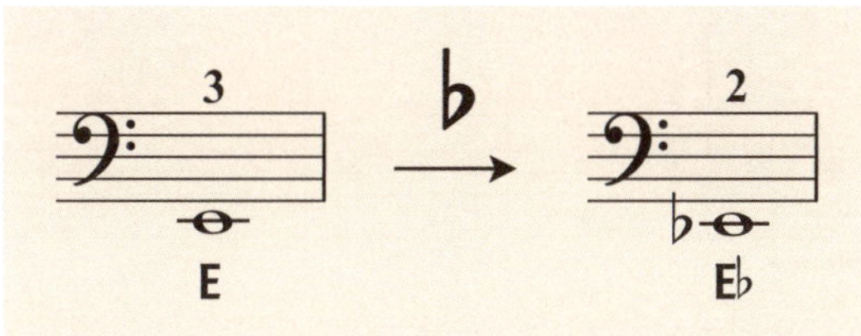

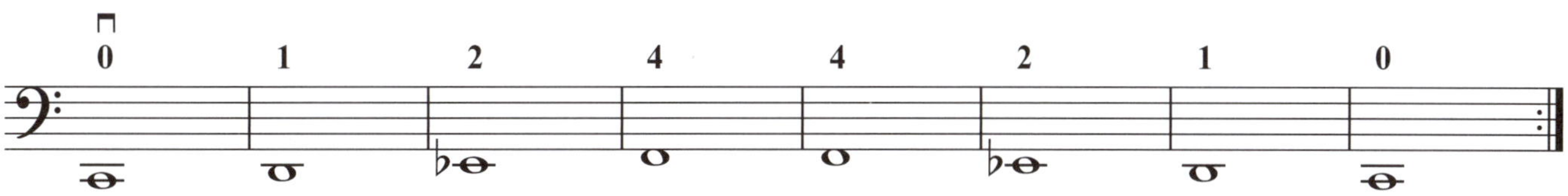

Baroque

Anonymous German manuscript
(around 2010)

Repeat the piece 'Going for a Walk' from page 59 and play it on the C string.

Swing-o-matic

G. K.

Exercises

Write out these notes on the G string

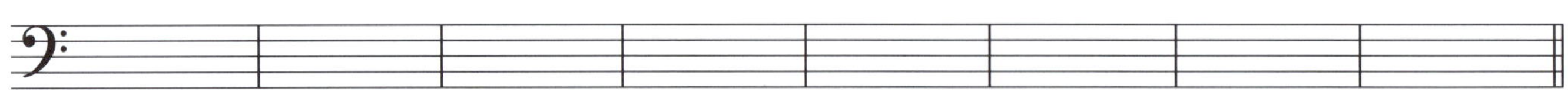

G B A B♭ C B A B♭

Write out these notes on the C string

C F E E♭ D E F E♭

Name these notes and write fingerings above them

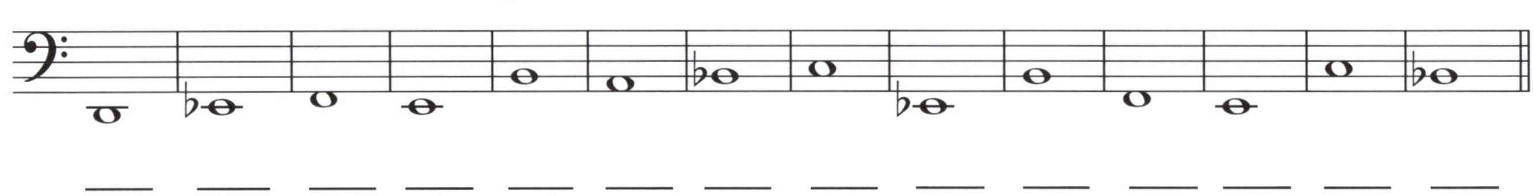

Track 66/67

Cross-country Boogie

G. K.

Staccato

Notes with a dot above or below the note head should be played very short: in musical language this is called *staccato*. Play jerkily, with energy and stop the bow again quietly. Be careful, though! When you stop, don't 'bite' into the string.

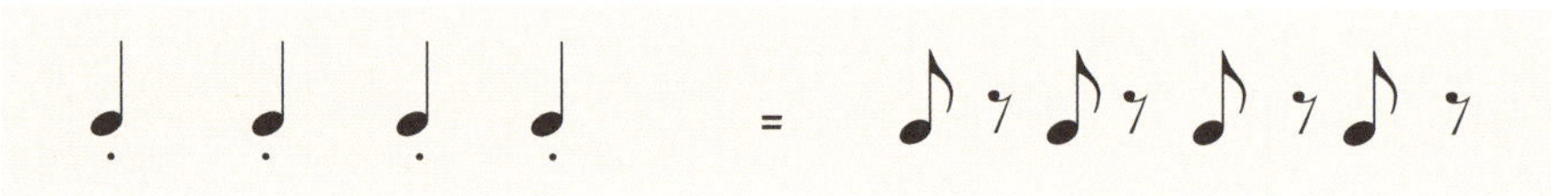

Exercises

𝄌 Coda sign: the last time through, jump from this sign to the coda sign at the end.

Track 68/69 **The Champion**

G. K.

Da Capo al 𝄌 - 𝄌

D 3rd cello part

Crescendo and decrescendo

crescendo (abbr. *cresc.*) = getting gradually louder

decrescendo (abbr. *decresc.*) = getting gradually softer

Track 70/71 **Surprise Symphony**

Joseph Haydn (1732–1809)
Arr.: Gabriel Koeppen

T Tune book p. 30

L No repeat on full version; playback with repeat

D Piano part

Track 72

Jam track 5: Weekend Cowboy

Now we juggle 6 balls – or rather notes - at once. It's quite easy, because the fingering is the same on D and A strings.

For example

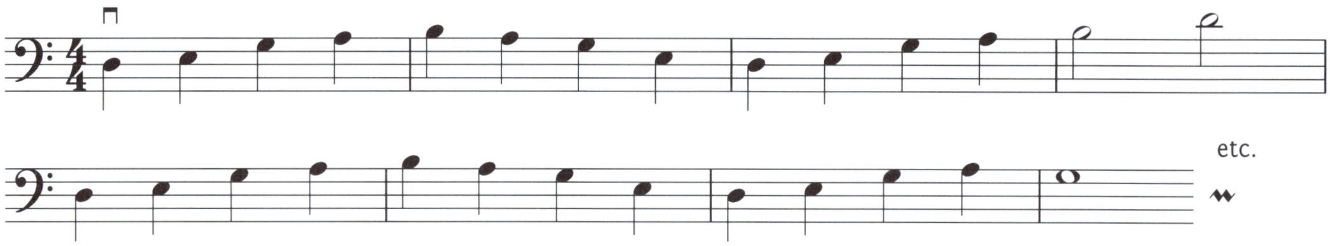

Keep playing freely using these notes:

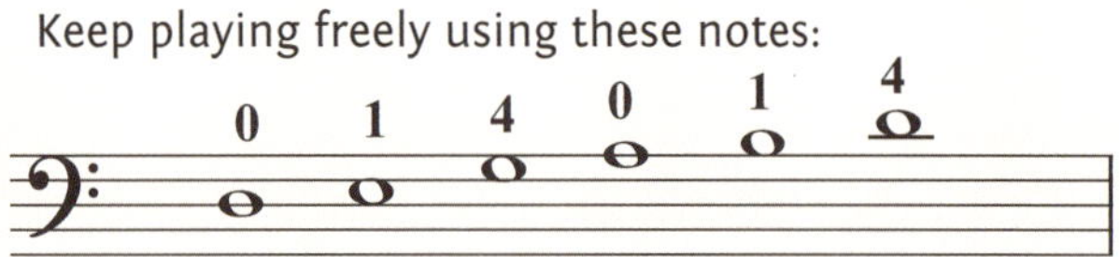

Write a piece of your own and play along with the jam track:

Name of the piece

Composer

Accompaniment:

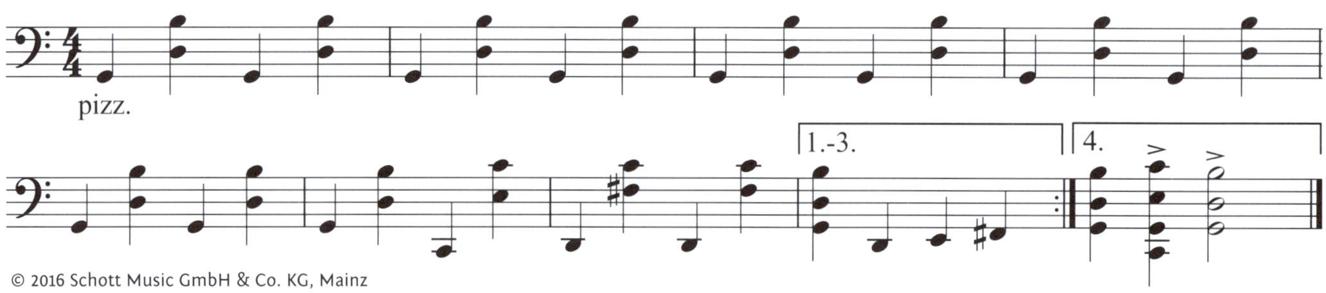

Dotted quarter notes (dotted crotchets)

A dot after a quarter note (crotchet) lengthens it by half its value again, for example by an extra eighth note (quaver):

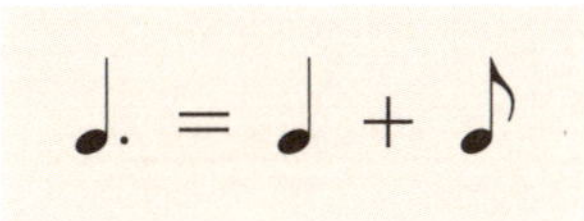

Busy

G. K.

Play arco, too

Song to the Sun

G. K.

Da Capo al Fine

Track 73/74 Ode to Joy

Ludwig van Beethoven
(1770–1827)

T Tune book p. 31

D Piano part

She'll Be Coming Round The Mountain

Traditional
Arr.: G. K.

D Piano part

Write out two octaves of the C major scale:

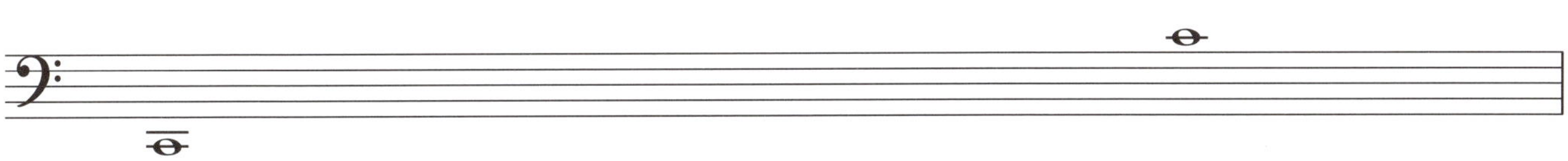

from C ——————————→ to C

Track 75/76

Up and Down

G. Koeppen

f
strumming
sim.
strumming
sim.
mf
f

Seaman's Blues

Swing ♩ = 104

G. Koeppen

Tune book p. 36

See you again in Book 2!

Bowings and alternative bowings for scales

Bowings for broken chords

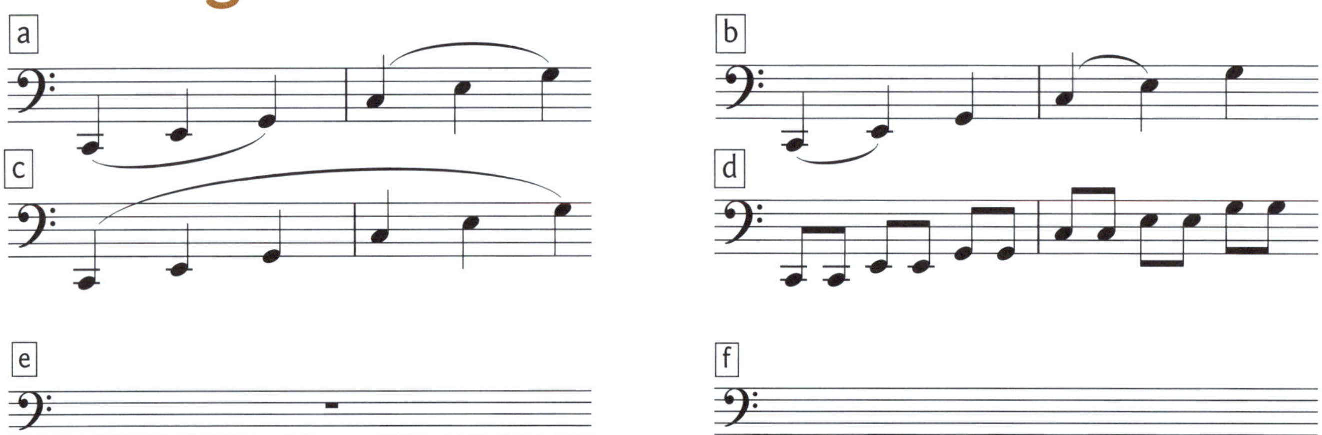

Manuscript paper for writing your own notes

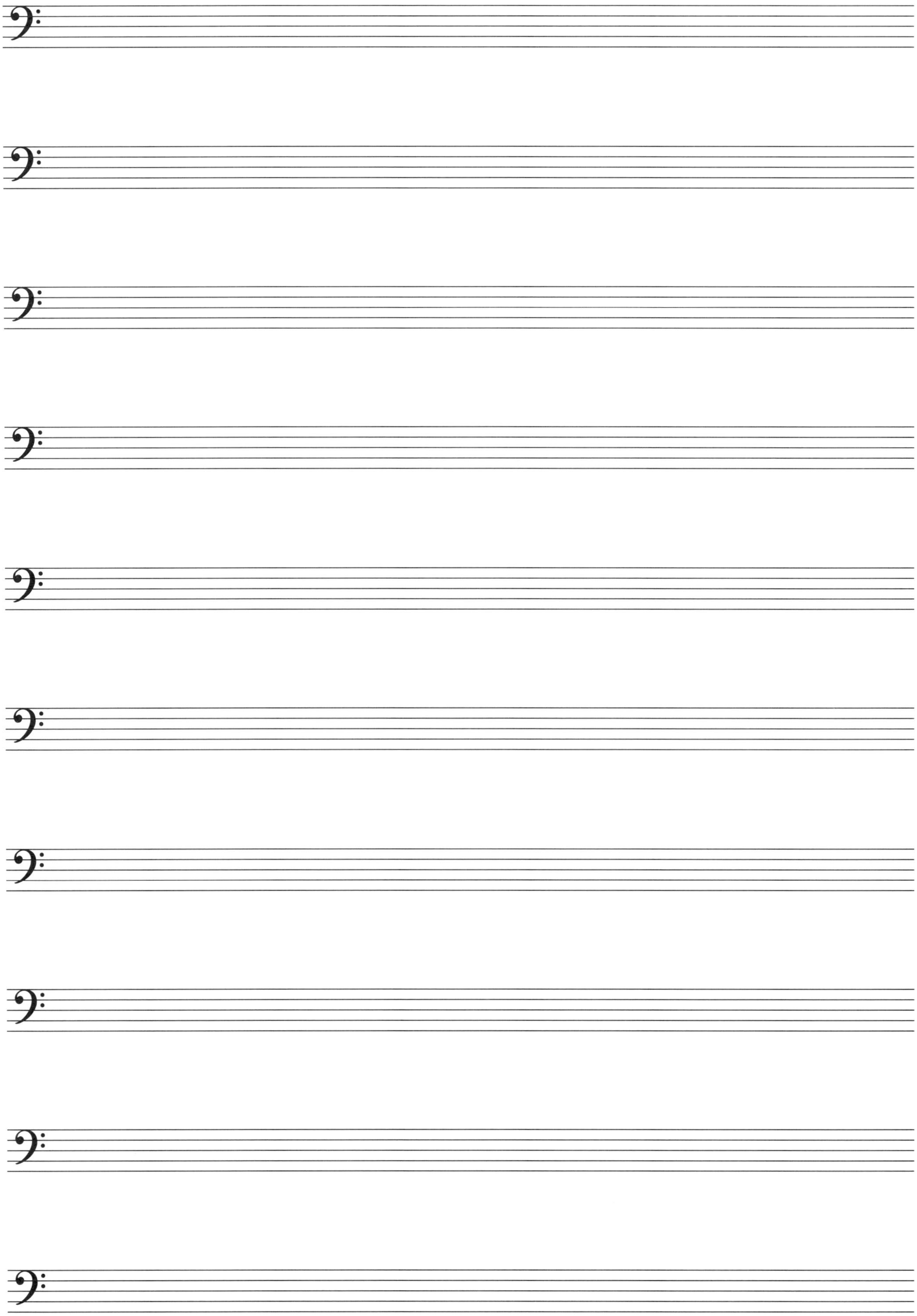

Tracklist

Track	title
1	Thoughtful
2	Waking up
3	One-note rock
4	Little March
5	Jam track 1: let's build a piece
6/7	Skip to my Lou
8/9	Lullaby
10/11	Tom Dooley
12/13	First Rock
14/15	Waiting
16/17	Rain song
18/19	Don't Tell Me Lies
20	Playing by ear
21/22	Catch me if you can!
23/24	In the desert
25/26	Robot
27/28	Party time
29/30	Keep going
31/32	Consolation
33/34	Dance of the Vikings
35	Jam track 2: Rocking Strings
36/37	Lucky Fellow
38/39	Swanee River
40/41	The Fat Hippopotamus
42/43	Eighths Boogie
44/45	Old MacDonald Had A Farm
46/47	Missing You
48	Jam track 3: Ballad
49/50	Little Brown Jug
51	Jam track 4: Mish-mash in ¾
52/53	Morning Has Broken
54/55	Elegy
56/57	French Song
58/59	Allemande
60/61	Vltava
62/63	Longing
64/65	Rainy City Blues
66/67	Cross-country Boogie
68/69	The Champion
70/71	Surprise Symphony
72	Jam track 5: Weekend Cowboy
73/74	Ode to Joy
75/76	Up and down
77	tuning note A (= 442 Hz)
78	tuning note D
79	tuning note G
80	tuning note C

The second number refers to the play-along version.
In the first five pieces you can play along with the full version.